Therapy and Counseling

**Recent Titles in
Q&A Health Guides**

THERAPY AND COUNSELING

Your Questions Answered

Christine L. B. Selby

Q&A Health Guides

An Imprint of ABC-CLIO, LLC
Santa Barbara, California • Denver, Colorado

Library of Congress Cataloging-in-Publication Data

Names: Selby, Christine L. B., author.
Title: Therapy and counseling : your questions answered / Christine L. B. Selby.
Description: Santa Barbara, CA : Greenwood, an Imprint of ABC-CLIO, LLC, [2019] |
    Series: Q&A health guides | Includes bibliographical references and index.
Identifiers: LCCN 2018056518 (print) | LCCN 2018057916 (ebook) |
    ISBN 9781440861680 (ebook) | ISBN 9781440861673 (print : alk. paper)
Subjects: LCSH: Psychotherapy—Miscellanea. | Counseling—Miscellanea.
Classification: LCC RC480.5 (ebook) | LCC RC480.5 .S4168 2019 (print) |
    DDC 616.89/14—dc23
LC record available at https://lccn.loc.gov/2018056518

ISBN: 978-1-4408-6167-3 (print)
       978-1-4408-6168-0 (ebook)

23 22 21 20 19   1 2 3 4 5

This book is also available as an eBook.

Greenwood
An Imprint of ABC-CLIO, LLC

ABC-CLIO, LLC
147 Castilian Drive
Santa Barbara, California 93117
www.abc-clio.com

This book is printed on acid-free paper ∞

Manufactured in the United States of America

This book is dedicated to all those who seek to better their lives by taking care of both their mind and body.

Contents

Series Foreword

All of us have questions about our health. Is this normal? Should I be doing something differently? Whom should I talk to about my concerns? And our modern world is full of answers. Thanks to the Internet, there's a wealth of information at our fingertips, from forums where people can share their personal experiences to Wikipedia articles to the full text of medical studies. But finding the right information can be an intimidating and difficult task—some sources are written at too high a level, others have been oversimplified, while still others are heavily biased or simply inaccurate.

Q&A Health Guides address the needs of readers who want accurate, concise answers to their health questions, authored by reputable and objective experts, and written in clear and easy-to-understand language. This series focuses on the topics that matter most to young adult readers, including various aspects of physical and emotional well-being as well as other components of a healthy lifestyle. These guides will also serve as a valuable tool for parents, school counselors, and others who may need to answer teens' health questions.

All books in the series follow the same format to make finding information quick and easy. Each volume begins with an essay on health literacy and why it is so important when it comes to gathering and evaluating health information. Next, the top five myths and misconceptions that surround the topic are dispelled. The heart of each guide is a collection of questions and answers, organized thematically. A selection of five case studies provides real-world examples to illuminate key concepts. Rounding out each volume are a directory of resources, glossary, and index. It is our hope that the books in this series will not only provide valuable information but will also help guide readers toward a lifetime of healthy decision making.

Acknowledgments

Many thanks to all those at ABC-CLIO who helped get this book to the version you are reading now. Special thanks to Maxine Taylor for offering me this project and for all of the invaluable feedback she provided me along the way.

Given the topic of this book, I would like to thank all of my professors and supervisors who helped illuminate for me the power of psychotherapy and instill in me the importance of ensuring that I am the best version of myself when helping others become the best version of themselves. And I would like to thank the myriad patients I have worked with over the years who have and continue to challenge me intellectually and interpersonally. Without them this version of this book would not exist.

Finally, and as always, I would like to thank my husband and my sons. This book would not exist without their support. Although my sons have a ways to go before they definitively decide what career path they will take, they both have expressed an interest in studying psychology. This has led me to view psychology through the lens of someone just learning about it and discovering how psychology can offer answers to many of life's more difficult questions and solutions to many of life's most challenging problems. My husband has been an exceptional business partner and consultant helping me see my life and my work from a different perspective. More important, he has been the kind of life partner who has, by his very existence, made me a better person than I was before I met him.

Introduction

This book covers many questions I get asked as a practicing psychotherapist and as a college professor teaching in the field of psychology. There are also many questions that I think more people would benefit from asking before deciding on a counselor or therapist. The mental health field is broad, in that there are clinicians who have varying types and amounts of training. This can, in many ways, directly impact whether a particular counselor or therapist will be a good fit for a particular patient.

Licensed counselors and therapists have not only different types of education but also different letters after their name (e.g., PhD, PsyD, LMFT, LCSW), which can make figuring out which counselor or therapist to work with confusing at best. In addition, even those with the same letters after their name may practice in very different ways. Some may approach mental health issues from a solution-focused perspective, whereas others may take an insight-oriented perspective. Knowing which among the myriad approaches to treatment will work best for you can be difficult to determine.

The objective of this book is to answer common questions that many people ask prior to setting up an appointment (e.g., how much does therapy cost?) as well as other questions that are important to know the answer to but may not cross the mind of someone looking for a counselor or therapist (e.g., do I need to see a counselor who has a particular specialty?). Specifically, the book starts with discussing myths associated with counseling and therapy and then specifically answers questions related to deciding whether you need counseling or therapy and how therapy works, questions about different types of therapy, questions about how to find a counselor and issues related to what happens once you're in counseling, and questions about how to access health insurance when you get mental health services. Finally, the book ends with case examples of people seeking or in therapy, a glossary of terms, and directory of resources that may be helpful to readers.

A couple of final notes. Although the terms "counselor" and "therapist" (and "counseling" and "therapy") are defined within the book, I have chosen to use these terms interchangeably since most people seeking mental health services do not make a distinction between counselor and therapist or counseling and therapy. In addition, I use the terms "patient" and "client" interchangeably. Although the term "client" is usually the term used in the context of counseling and therapy, the use of the term "patient" is also used. "Client" refers to someone using a professional's services, and "patient" refers to someone receiving treatment; thus both are appropriate in this context.

I hope this book enlightens readers about how therapy works and how to find a counselor or therapist. After all, when it comes to your mental well-being, it is important to be sure that you get the best help available to you.

Guide to Health Literacy

On her 13th birthday, Samantha was diagnosed with type 2 diabetes. She consulted her mom and her aunt, both of whom also have type 2 diabetes, and decided to go with their strategy of managing diabetes by taking insulin. As a result of participating in an after-school program at her middle school that focused on health literacy, she learned that she can help manage the level of glucose in her bloodstream by counting her carbohydrate intake, following a diabetic diet, and exercising regularly. But, what exactly should she do? How does she keep track of her carbohydrate intake? What is a diabetic diet? How long should she exercise and what type of exercise should she do? Samantha is a visual learner, so she turned to her favorite source of media, YouTube, to answer these questions. She found videos from individuals around the world sharing their experiences and tips, doctors (or at least people who have "Dr." in their YouTube channel names), government agencies such as the National Institutes of Health, and even video clips from cat lovers who have cats with diabetes. With guidance from the librarian and the health and science teachers at her school, she assessed the credibility of the information in these videos and even compared their suggestions to some of the print resources that she was able to find at her school library. Now, she knows exactly how to count her carbohydrate level, how to prepare and follow a diabetic diet, and how much (and what) exercise is needed daily. She intends to share her findings with her mom and her aunt, and now she wants to create a chart that summarizes what she has learned that she can share with her doctor.

Samantha's experience is not unique. She represents a shift in our society; an individual no longer views himself or herself as a passive recipient of medical care but as an active mediator of his or her own health. However, in this era when any individual can post his or her opinions and experiences with a particular health condition online with just a few clicks or publish a memoir, it is vital that people know how to assess the credibility of health information. Gone are the days when "publishing" health information required intense vetting. The health information landscape is highly saturated, and people have innumerable sources where they can find information about practically any health topic. The sources (whether print, online, or a person) that an individual consults for health information are crucial because the accuracy and trustworthiness of the information can potentially affect his or her overall health. The ability to find, select, assess, and use health information constitutes a type of literacy—health literacy—that everyone must possess.

THE DEFINITION AND PHASES OF HEALTH LITERACY

One of the most popular definitions for health literacy comes from Ratzan and Parker (2000), who describe health literacy as "the degree to which individuals have the capacity to obtain, process, and understand basic health information and services needed to make appropriate health decisions." Recent research has extrapolated health literacy into health literacy bits, further shedding light on the multiple phases and literacy practices that are embedded within the multifaceted concept of health literacy. Although this research has focused primarily on online health information seeking, these health literacy bits are needed to successfully navigate both print and online sources. There are six phases of health information seeking: (1) Information Need Identification and Question Formulation, (2) Information Search, (3) Information Comprehension, (4) Information Assessment, (5) Information Management, and (6) Information Use.

The first phase is the *information need identification and question formulation phase*. In this phase, one needs to be able to develop and refine a range of questions to frame one's search and understand relevant health terms. In the second phase, *information search*, one has to possess appropriate searching skills, such as using proper keywords and correct spelling in search terms, especially when using search engines and databases. It is also crucial to understand how search engines work (i.e., how search results are derived, what the order of the search results means, how to use the snippets that are provided in the search results list to select websites, and how to determine which listings are ads on a search engine results page). One also has to limit reliance on surface characteristics, such as the design of a website or a book (a website or book that appears to have a lot of information or looks aesthetically pleasant does not necessarily mean it has good information) and language used (a website or book that utilizes jargon, the keywords that one used to conduct the search, or the word "information" does not necessarily indicate it will have good information). The next phase is *information comprehension*, whereby one needs to have the ability to read, comprehend, and recall the information (including textual, numerical, and visual content) one has located from the books and/or online resources.

To assess the credibility of health information (*information assessment* phase), one needs to be able to evaluate information for accuracy, evaluate how current the information is (e.g., when a website was last updated or when a book was published), and evaluate the creators of the source—for example, examine site sponsors or type of sites (.com, .gov, .edu, or .org) or the author of a book (practicing doctor, a celebrity doctor, a patient of a specific disease, etc.) to determine the believability of the person/ organization providing the information. Such credibility perceptions tend to become generalized, so they must be frequently reexamined (e.g., the belief that a specific news agency always has credible health information needs continuous vetting). One also needs to evaluate the credibility of the medium (e.g., television, Internet, radio, social media, and book) and evaluate—not just accept without questioning—others' claims regarding the validity of a site, book, or other specific source of information. At this stage, one has to "make sense of information gathered from diverse sources by identifying misconceptions, main and supporting ideas, conflicting information, point of view, and biases" (American Association of School Librarians [AASL], 2009, p. 13) and conclude which sources/ information are valid and accurate by using conscious strategies rather than simply using intuitive judgments or "rules of thumb." This phase is the most challenging segment of health information seeking and serves as a determinant of success (or lack thereof) in the information-seeking process. The following section on Sources of Health Information further explains this phase.

The fifth phase is *information management*, whereby one has to organize information that has been gathered in some manner to ensure easy retrieval and use in the future. The last phase is *information use*, in which one will synthesize information found across various resources, draw conclusions, and locate the answer to his or her original question and/or the content that fulfills the information need. This phase also often involves implementation, such as using the information to solve a health problem; make health-related decisions; identify and engage in behaviors that will help a person to avoid health risks; share the health information found with family members and friends who may benefit from it; and advocate more broadly for personal, family, or community health.

THE IMPORTANCE OF HEALTH LITERACY

The conception of health has moved from a passive view (someone is either well or ill) to one that is more active and process based (someone is working toward preventing or managing disease). Hence, the dominant focus has shifted from doctors and treatments to patients and prevention, resulting in the need to strengthen our ability and confidence (as patients and consumers of health care) to look for, assess, understand, manage, share, adapt, and use health-related information. An individual's health literacy level has been found to predict his or her health status better than age, race, educational attainment, employment status, and income level (National Network of Libraries of Medicine, 2013). Greater health literacy also enables individuals to better communicate with health care providers such as doctors, nutritionists, and therapists, as they can pose more relevant, informed, and useful questions to health care providers. Another added advantage of greater health literacy is better information-seeking skills, not only for health but also in other domains, such as completing assignments for school.

SOURCES OF HEALTH INFORMATION: THE GOOD, THE BAD, AND THE IN-BETWEEN

For generations, doctors, nurses, nutritionists, health coaches, and other health professionals have been the trusted sources of health information. Additionally, researchers have found that young adults, when they have health-related questions, typically turn to a family member who has had firsthand experience with a health condition because of their family member's close proximity and because of their past experience with, and trust in, this individual. Expertise should be a core consideration when consulting a person, website, or book for health information. The credentials and background of the person or author and conflicting interests of the author (and his or her organization) must be checked and validated to ensure the likely credibility of the health information they are conveying. While books often have implied credibility because of the peer-review process involved, self-publishing has challenged this credibility, so qualifications of book authors should also be verified. When it comes to health information, currency of the source must also be examined. When examining health information/studies presented, pay attention to the exhaustiveness of research methods utilized to offer recommendations or conclusions. Small and nondiverse sample size is often—but not always—an indication of reduced credibility. Studies that confuse correlation with causation is another potential issue to watch for. Information seekers must also pay attention to the sponsors of the research studies. For example, if a study is sponsored by manufacturers of drug Y and the study recommends that drug Y is the best treatment to manage or cure a disease, this may indicate a lack of objectivity on the part of the researchers.

The Internet is rapidly becoming one of the main sources of health information. Online forums, news agencies, personal blogs, social media sites, pharmacy sites, and celebrity "doctors" are all offering medical and health information targeted to various types of people in regard to all types of diseases and symptoms. There are professional journalists, citizen journalists, hoaxers, and people paid to write fake health news on various sites that may appear to have a legitimate domain name and may even have authors who claim to have professional credentials, such as an MD. All these sites *may* offer useful information or information that appears to be useful and relevant; however, much of the information may be debatable and may fall into gray areas that require readers to discern credibility, reliability, and biases.

While broad recognition and acceptance of certain media, institutions, and people often serve as the most popular determining factors to assess credibility of health information among young people, keep in mind that there are legitimate Internet sites, databases, and books that publish health information and serve as sources of health information for doctors, other health sites, and members of the public. For example, MedlinePlus (https://medlineplus.gov) has trusted sources on over 975 diseases and conditions and presents the information in easy-to-understand language.

The chart here presents factors to consider when assessing credibility of health information. However, keep in mind that these factors function only as a guide and require continuous updating to keep abreast with the changes in the landscape of health information, information sources, and technologies.

The chart can serve as a guide; however, approaching a librarian about how one can go about assessing the credibility of both print

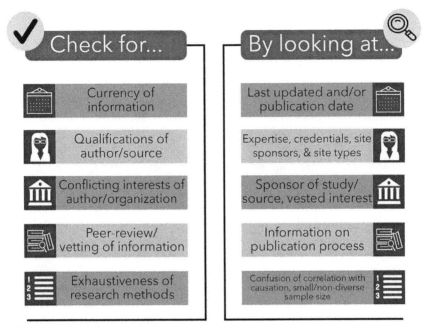

All images from flaticon.com

and online health information is far more effective than using generic checklist-type tools. While librarians are not health experts, they can apply and teach patrons strategies to determine the credibility of health information.

With the prevalence of fake sites and fake resources that appear to be legitimate, it is important to use the following health information assessment tips to verify health information that one has obtained (St. Jean et al., 2015, p. 151):

- **Don't assume you are right**: Even when you feel very sure about an answer, keep in mind that the answer may not be correct, and it is important to conduct (further) searches to validate the information.
- **Don't assume you are wrong**: You may actually have correct information, even if the information you encounter does not match—that is, you may be right and the resources that you have found may contain false information.
- **Take an open approach**: Maintain a critical stance by not including your preexisting beliefs as keywords (or letting them influence your choice of keywords) in a search, as this may influence what it is possible to find out.

- **Verify, verify, and verify**: Information found, especially on the Internet, needs to be validated, no matter how the information appears on the site (i.e., regardless of the appearance of the site or the quantity of information that is included).

Health literacy comes with experience navigating health information. Professional sources of health information, such as doctors, health care providers, and health databases, are still the best, but one also has the power to search for health information and then verify it by consulting with these trusted sources and by using the health information assessment tips and guide shared previously.

Mega Subramaniam, PhD
Associate Professor, College of Information
Studies, University of Maryland

REFERENCES AND FURTHER READING

American Association of School Librarians (AASL). (2009). *Standards for the 21st-century learner in action.* Chicago, IL: American Association of School Librarians.

Hilligoss, B., & Rieh, S.-Y. (2008). Developing a unifying framework of credibility assessment: Construct, heuristics, and interaction in context. *Information Processing & Management, 44*(4), 1467–1484.

Kuhlthau, C. C. (1988). Developing a model of the library search process: Cognitive and affective aspects. *Reference Quarterly, 28*(2), 232–242.

National Network of Libraries of Medicine (NNLM). (2013). Health literacy. Bethesda, MD: National Network of Libraries of Medicine. Retrieved from nnlm.gov/outreach/consumer/hlthlit.html

Ratzan, S. C., & Parker, R. M. (2000). Introduction. In C. R. Selden, M. Zorn, S. C. Ratzan, & R. M. Parker (Eds.), *National Library of Medicine current bibliographies in medicine: Health literacy.* NLM Pub. No. CBM 2000-1. Bethesda, MD: National Institutes of Health, U.S. Department of Health and Human Services.

St. Jean, B., Subramaniam, M., Taylor, N. G., Follman, R., Kodama, C., & Casciotti, D. (2015). The influence of positive hypothesis testing on youths' online health-related information seeking. *New Library World, 116*(3/4), 136–154.

St. Jean, B., Taylor, N. G., Kodama, C., & Subramaniam, M. (February 2017). Assessing the health information source perceptions of tweens using card-sorting exercises. *Journal of Information Science*, April 2018, 44(2), 148–164. Retrieved from http://journals.sagepub.com/doi/abs/ 10.1177/0165551516687728

Subramaniam, M., St. Jean, B., Taylor, N. G., Kodama, C., Follman, R., & Casciotti, D. (2015). Bit by bit: Using design-based research to improve the health literacy of adolescents. *JMIR Research Protocols*, 4(2), paper e62. Retrieved from http://www.ncbi.nlm.nih.gov/pmc/ articles/PMC4464334/

Valenza, J. (2016, November 26). Truth, truthiness, and triangulation: A news literacy toolkit for a "post-truth" world [Web log]. Retrieved from http://blogs.slj.com/neverendingsearch/2016/11/26/truth-truthi ness-triangulation-and-the-librarian-way-a-news-literacy-toolkit-for-a-post-truth-world/

---❖---

Common Misconceptions about Therapy and Counseling

1. MY PROBLEMS AREN'T SEVERE ENOUGH TO NEED COUNSELING

This is a common concern among many people who consider seeking counseling. Some people fear they will be wasting their time and the counselor's time if their problems aren't that serious. This may further leave them feeling embarrassed or ashamed. Others may consider their symptoms not that serious because they are not "crazy" and therefore do not need counseling. The reality is that many people who need counseling do not seek services for these and other reasons. As a result their problems go untreated and have the possibility of getting worse and therefore more difficult to treat. By thinking that your problems aren't serious enough and that you'll be wasting everyone's time you risk minimizing your struggles and prevent yourself from getting help for something that is likely easier treated the sooner it is identified. Similarly, those who think they are not crazy and therefore don't need counseling also run the risk of their symptoms worsening, which become more difficult to treat as more time passes. Anyone can benefit from counseling or therapy regardless of the seriousness of their concerns. Moreover, since we are generally not very good judges of our own behavior, it is a good idea to let a licensed mental health professional determine if a formal diagnosis is necessary and what forms of treatment may be most effective. For more information about when to seek counseling, see Question 1, Questions 3 and 4 for information on differences between professionals and their credentials, and Questions 7–19 for information on different types of therapy.

2. MEDICATION IS THE FASTEST AND MOST EFFECTIVE WAY TO DEAL WITH MENTAL HEALTH ISSUES

It is quite common for people diagnosed with a mental illness to be prescribed a psychotropic medication (i.e., a medication for a mental illness). In some cases medication for the mental illness may be the only form of treatment they receive. Others may benefit from taking a prescribed medication but may be worried that it will not help or may be hesitant to take it because of possible side effects. Still others may fear that taking a psychiatric medication means they are "crazy." Regardless of the reason someone may take or not take medication, it is not the fastest and most effective way to deal with mental health issues. Research shows that for most mental health diagnoses a combination of medication and counseling or therapy is the most effective course of treatment. Medications can be effective in ameliorating specific symptoms of some disorders, but they do not address the psychological causes or factors that maintain the disorder which are addressed in counseling or therapy. In our current society, we are used to fixing things as fast as possible after we identify a problem. In addition, many purely medical diseases have very specific cures (e.g., medication, surgery) that can be implemented as quickly as needed, and in many cases, relief from symptoms occurs within hours or days of treatment. Although it is possible and in some cases likely that people seeking counseling will feel some relief after the first session or two, depending on the nature and severity of the mental health issue, it will become clear rather quickly that the initial relief was temporary and more psychological work is needed before more long-lasting relief is possible. For more information on psychotropic medications and how long it may take to feel better in therapy, see Questions 34 and 29, respectively.

3. THERE IS A CERTAIN LENGTH OF TIME I'LL BE IN THERAPY

Unfortunately, it is not possible to predict with 100 percent certainty how long any given person will be in therapy. There are some courses of treatment that are time-limited because of the constraints of the facility (e.g., there is a high need so patients are allotted only a certain number of sessions regardless of their concern) or because there is a specific treatment protocol that outlines how long treatment will be and what will happen at each session. It is more common, however, for people seeking therapy to be seen the number of sessions it takes for them to feel the degree of relief they are looking for. It is reasonable to ask one's counselor or therapist how long they think therapy will take. Some counselors or therapists may correctly assert that given what they know about the person and their mental health concerns they also know that most people will feel better after a certain period of time. They are also likely to add that the length of treatment will vary from one person to another due to unexpected changes in symptoms (improvement or worsening), unforeseen crises arising, absence from treatment, and so on. For more information about what to expect in therapy and how long it may take, see Questions 27–29.

4. PEOPLE WHO I DON'T WANT TO KNOW ABOUT MY THERAPY WILL FIND OUT ABOUT IT

This is a common concern among people seeking mental health services whether they say it out loud to anyone or not. The fact is, however, your counselor or therapist is bound by law and by their professional ethics to keep confidential what happens in therapy sessions. A therapist cannot reveal anything about their work with you, which includes the fact that you are seeking therapy services, unless you provide them written permission in the form of a release of information (ROI). The only way anyone will know you are working with a counselor is if you tell them you are. There are some exceptions to this, however. In the case of a minor, depending on the minor's age, the parents are the ones who provide (or not) permission for the counselor to reveal whether their child is in counseling and what is being addressed. Additional exceptions to this include whether you are an imminent danger to yourself (i.e., suicide) or someone else (e.g., threatening to seriously harm someone else) and if you are court ordered for mental health treatment. In these cases the counselor has the ethical duty and legal right to inform someone else about the fact that you are working with them—though there are still limitations as to what can or should be revealed and who can or should be informed. For more information about the ROI, the confidentiality of your sessions, and what to do when others know you're seeking counseling, see Questions 26, 32, and 38, respectively, and Question 36 for information about HIPAA.

5. GOING TO COUNSELING MEANS I'VE GIVEN UP OR I'M WEAK

Although this is a concern for many who seek counseling, it may be more prevalent among males, especially those who are concerned about showing any sign of weakness. The culture of the United States very much supports the idea of strength and autonomy—that we can and should take care of things ourselves whenever possible. There are, in fact, numerous stories from politicians or celebrities who indicate that they "overcame" a mental health issue by sheer will and determination—the implication, of course, is that other people can too. While it is impossible to know what truth may exist in such claims, the reality is that going to counseling is often necessary to address and feel relief from mental health concerns. Fortunately, more and more celebrities have acknowledged the fact not only that they have had or are currently dealing with mental health issues but that they also sought professional assistance for their concerns. When well-known people speak out like this, it can help dissipate the stigma attached to seeking counseling. Regardless, the work done in counseling is often quite difficult and painful. It is common for people in counseling to feel worse before they feel better. Thus, it takes a great deal of strength to not only identify that one needs help but also persist in seeking help despite the pain one experiences as part of the process. Seeking counseling does not mean one has given up; it simply means that what one has tried to do in order to feel better has not worked and that one needs someone with a particular type of expertise to help find a way through one's mental health concerns. For more information about how to figure out when you need counseling or therapy, what to expect when you start, and how to handle concerns about your counselor's or others' perception of you, see Questions 1, 2, 6, and 38, respectively.

QUESTIONS AND ANSWERS

General Information

1. How do I know if I need counseling?

There is no hard-and-fast rule to help people determine whether they need counseling; however, it is possible to figure it out in a variety of ways, each of which does require keeping an open mind. This is especially true if you find you are at all resistant to counseling in general or if you think that your problems are not that bad. The following are some questions you can ask yourself. It may be helpful to write your thoughts and reactions to each question on a piece of paper.

1. Do you think there are any concerns to address?

If you answered "yes" to this question, then the answer to the original question is that counseling would likely be beneficial for you. If you are not sure whether you have concerns or issues that need to be addressed, your answers to the questions that follow may help clarify your answer.

2. Has anyone in your life expressed concern for you?

Friends and family can see things not going well for each of us before we do. If a friend or family member has asked if you are okay or if there is something wrong, it is worth reflecting on why they might think there is. If you are simply overtired, for example, or have had a rough day, then that may explain their concern. If, however, you are consistently tired or consistently have rough days, then this may be a reason to seek counseling to try to figure out what you need to do to prevent yourself from, at best, having a low quality of life and, at worst, living an unhealthy life.

If you are unable to identify why it may appear to your friends or family that you are struggling, it is a good idea to ask them why they think there might be something wrong. Their answer may spark in you a realization that things are not going as well for you as you thought and seeking counseling may be a good idea. Alternatively, their response may leave you unsure why you may look upset, sad, or unhealthy to them. For example, if they say "I don't know, you just look like something is wrong," it may still be beneficial to seek counseling so you can discern what may be going on.

3. How long have you been dealing with your current concerns?

If you know you are struggling, another way to determine if counseling is a good idea for you is to think about how long you have been struggling (which can include how long you have been overtired, for example, or having rough days). The longer something is going on, the more likely it is that counseling would be helpful. This is especially true if you have tried a variety of solutions to fix what you're struggling with and nothing seems to work. Ideally, seeking a counselor before you get to the point where you feel like "this is just the way life is" or "there is nothing I can do about it" is best.

There is no specific length of time you should wait or that you have to wait before you seek counseling. In fact, many counselors might suggest that the moment you wonder if counseling would be helpful is the perfect time to set up an appointment since, at some level, you know that things aren't going great, and figuring out why that is, as early as possible, gives you a much greater chance of preventing your concerns from becoming worse.

4. Do you have more than one concern?

It is possible that if you have more than one concern, there is still one overarching problem that is affecting many areas of your life. For example, you may be working so many hours that you are exhausted and irritable, which in turn has affected your friendships and/or dating relationships. Alternatively, having more than one concern may indicate that you are dealing with more than one issue or more than one mental health diagnosis. For example, you may feel like you are sad a lot, and at other times you are anxious and you are struggling to manage these feelings. Or you may feel sad or anxious most of the time and have found a way to manage your feelings by using alcohol or other substances, thereby relying on substances to feel better. Having more than one area of concern suggests that more of your life may be negatively impacted, which increases the possibility that things will feel worse more quickly or more intensely than if only one area of your life is affected.

5. How are your current concerns affecting you (i.e., how are they interfering with your life)?

A hallmark of mental health issues and ultimately the need for mental health treatment is whether what you're dealing with interferes with your life in any way. As noted in the answer to the previous question, when multiple areas of your life are negatively impacted, your problems may get worse faster, or they can make you feel worse because more areas of your life are affected. Regardless of how many areas of your life are affected, even if only one area is negatively affected, this is a good indication that counseling may be not only beneficial but also necessary. Although many people with mental health issues who do not receive treatment do get better, research shows that those who seek mental health treatment are more likely to get better and they get better more quickly compared to those who do not seek treatment.

Thus, if you realize that your current concerns negatively impact any of the following areas of your life, it is a good idea to seek counseling as soon as possible.

- Friendships
- Dating relationships
- Relationships with family members
- Work and/or school (e.g., you consistently get into trouble for coming in late, not getting your work done)
- Your concerns result in getting into trouble with the law (e.g., you got arrested for public intoxication)
- Your finances are negatively impacted by your current concerns (e.g., you are overspending to make yourself feel better)

6. Do you have people in your life who are trustworthy and supportive?

One of the things often considered when assisting people in counseling is the degree to which they have a good social support system.

What matters so much is not how many people are in your life but the quality of those relationships. For example, you may have a lot of people you consider friends but you also know that there isn't anyone in whom you'd confide if you were having a hard time. By contrast, you may have only one person you consider important to you but you know you can count on them to be there for you, to listen to you, and to help you in whatever way they can. Having a good social support system does not mean you don't need counseling, but the lack of a good social support system is a more clear indication that counseling is a good idea. Going to counseling under those circumstances not only provides you with a safe place to talk about what you need to, but it may also help you develop relationships with others who are trustworthy and who are supportive.

When in doubt you can always schedule a session with a counselor for the expressed purpose of helping you decide if you need counseling. Some counselors can help you figure that out via a brief phone conversation; however, it is more likely that they will recommend a more thorough conversation via a scheduled appointment so they have a chance to get to know you a bit and what your current concerns are. Scheduling such an appointment will also afford you the opportunity to ask questions about any concerns you have about seeking counseling, such as whether your problems are "serious enough," how long counseling may take before you start to feel better, and so on.

2. In general, how does therapy work?

This question is a bit more complicated than it may sound because how counseling or therapy works depends, in part, on the type of counseling you receive (see Questions 7–19 for more information on the most common types of counseling); however, there are enough commonalities between the various forms of counseling and therapy to address this question adequately. In the most basic terms, therapy works by the therapist first assessing your concerns, determining if a formal diagnosis is appropriate, and engaging in treatment based on the therapist's current understanding of the issues.

Depending on the therapist you have, the assessment may be more or less formal. An initial assessment usually takes the form of a clinical interview during which specific questions are asked in order to get as clear a picture as possible of what your concerns are and how they affect you.

This type of interview can be *structured, semi-structured,* or *unstructured.* A structured interview involves a specific set of questions, all of which are asked in a particular order. A semi-structured interview involves a set of questions, all of which are asked, but the therapist may ask follow-up questions based on your answers. By contrast, an unstructured interview involves the therapist asking generally what your concerns are or what made you decide to seek counseling. Based on your answers, the therapist will ask additional questions to help clarify their understanding of your concerns and how they affect you. Oftentimes, the clinical interview takes place during one session; however, it is possible that a second and possibly a third session may be required to gather all of the information needed to ensure the therapist's understanding of your concerns is as clear as possible. This is important so the therapist can make an accurate diagnosis. If needed, the therapist may have you complete a questionnaire designed to gather information about a specific issue. For example, the therapist may ask you to complete a questionnaire designed to measure your level of depression or anxiety or a questionnaire designed to determine whether you are dealing with thoughts of suicide. Sometimes the therapist may make a referral to a psychologist who specializes in psychological testing (see Question 33 for more information on psychological testing) in order to further clarify the nature of your concerns and appropriate diagnosis.

Once the assessment has been completed, there should be enough information for your therapist to determine if a mental health diagnosis is appropriate and if so which one(s). In the United States a diagnosis is made using a manual titled the *Diagnostic and Statistical Manual of Mental Disorders* (DSM). The most recent edition, published in 2013, is referred to as the *DSM-5.* This manual is used by licensed mental health professionals to identify the correct diagnosis. The manual itself contains not only the specific criteria or symptoms that must be met for each diagnosis but also information such as who is usually diagnosed with the particular disorder (e.g., males/females, children/adults), what other disorders may share similar symptoms and therefore must be *ruled out,* and what other disorders are likely to be diagnosed along with the disorder in question. The manual also contains a summary of how common the disorder is, when it usually develops, what may put someone at risk for developing the disorder, cultural issues that may affect the diagnosis of the disorder, and possible consequences of having the disorder.

Accurate assessment and diagnosis of a patient's concerns is paramount since the nature and course of treatment are largely dependent

on the diagnosis itself. Once the appropriate form of treatment is identified, the therapist and patient will dive into the work of addressing
the current concerns. This will begin with identifying specific goals for
therapy, which may initially be as vague as wanting to feel better or as
specific as wanting particular symptoms to cease existing. Once the goals
are identified and agreed on, the therapy work may involve the therapist
teaching the client specific skills to deal with a symptom. For example,
someone dealing with anxiety may learn how to effectively use relaxation techniques as part of their daily life as well as during particularly
stressful circumstances that are likely to activate their anxiety. Someone
who is depressed may learn how to identify and counteract negative and
self-defeating thought patterns that contribute to their feelings of depression. It is possible, depending on the diagnosis as well as the severity of
the patient's symptoms, that the therapist may recommend the patient
seek prescription medication to help alleviate their symptoms (see Question 34 for more information on medication referrals). Therapy may
also involve allowing time for the patient to share their thoughts about
and reactions to how they are feeling that particular week. Although
this may be considered "venting," the reality is that sometimes talking
about daily struggles or particular distressing but temporary events can be
highly beneficial for people, especially when done with someone who is
nonjudgmental and empathic. Therapy may also involve talking about
long-standing patterns of behavior that seem to keep recurring and causing problems for the patient. In this case, it may be likely that the therapist will ask about these behaviors in the context of one's early years.
That is, the therapist may ask what it was like for the patient growing up;
what their relationships during that time were like with family members,
friends, and peers; and how those early experiences may be continuing to
affect them as an adolescent or adult.

As therapy progresses, patients may find they feel worse before they
feel better as they uncover more concerns than they previously thought
they had or learn something new about themselves that they may not
like. It is equally possible that patients will feel better immediately after
the first session (see Question 27 for more information about the first
session) since seeking counseling with a trained professional can often
be a relief and provide a sense of hope that things can get better. In addition, as the patient's concerns are addressed overtime, the patient will
likely feel better overall (see Question 29 for more information on how
long it may take to feel better). As therapy progresses the patient and
therapist will continue to work toward the goals they set for therapy—
including making adjustments to the goals as needed—and determine

together when the patient may be ready to space the sessions out or to stop counseling altogether.

3. What are the differences between a counselor, therapist, psychologist, and psychiatrist?

Some of these terms are generic, which can be used to describe any mental health professional. Some of these terms specifically denote the type of training the individual has received and, in some cases, specifically what they are allowed to do professionally.

The terms "counselor" and "therapist" (i.e., psychotherapist) are often used interchangeably. That is, patients may refer to the person with whom they are working as their counselor or their therapist. The term used is usually a personal preference or one that they are most familiar with. Both of these terms can refer to people who may be very different in terms of their background and training. The focus here, of course, is on professionals in the mental health field; however, a counselor can also refer to a school counselor, guidance counselor, or even a lawyer. A therapist can refer to a physical therapist, occupational therapist, or medication therapist. Although in real life the term you use (or the mental health professional uses) doesn't really matter, there are some important differences.

The term "counselor" often refers to someone who may offer advice or guidance as to a helpful course of action. A counselor is also likely to focus on current problems and symptoms with the intent to identify problem-solving strategies to address the current issues. By contrast, the term "therapist"—which is short for psychotherapist—will focus on insight into the current concerns. That is, a therapist will help the patient develop an understanding of why a particular issue has arisen (or keeps reappearing) with the understanding that determining why a problem exists can help the person more effectively address the current concern and prevent it from resurfacing again in the future. Your counselor or therapist may have a master's degree in counseling or social work or may have a doctoral degree in counseling, social work, psychology, or psychiatry (see Question 4 for more information on credentials).

The terms "psychologist" and "psychiatrist" are both legally protected terms, which means that only professionals with specific types of training can refer to themselves using one of these terms. A psychologist is typically a professional who has a doctoral degree (there are a few exceptions to this that vary by state and can mean that the psychologist has a master's degree in psychology). A doctoral degree in psychology is either a

PhD or PsyD. The primary difference between the two doctoral degrees has to do with how much knowledge and experience in understanding and conducting research the professional in training must have. The PhD degree requires more research compared to what is expected with the PsyD degree. Both PhD and PsyD require extensive training and supervision in counseling and/or psychotherapy. A psychologist is trained to diagnose and treat mental illness. A psychologist is also trained to conduct psychological assessments (see Question 33 for more information on psychological assessment) involving tools that measure IQ, learning disability, personality, symptoms related to specific diagnoses [e.g., depression, anxiety, attention-deficit/hyperactivity disorder (ADHD), autism spectrum], and so on. It is common for a psychologist to focus primarily on either diagnosing and treating mental illness or conducting psychological evaluations.

A psychiatrist is a physician by training and therefore has an MD degree with a specialty in psychiatry. Like the psychologist, a psychiatrist is trained to diagnose and treat mental illness, which may include counseling/psychotherapy or prescribing medication. Most psychiatrists focus on treatment via medication rather than counseling or psychotherapy (see Question 34 for more information on medication referrals). Some psychiatrists, however, provide both forms of treatment. Although psychiatrists are often the individuals who prescribe medication for mental illness, the reality is that others can as well. Psychiatric nurse practitioners, and primary care providers (e.g., a general practice physician or nurse), can prescribe, and in some states, psychologists are able to prescribe medication as long as they receive specific training to do so.

4. What credentials should I look for when choosing a counselor or therapist?

There are a wide variety of credentials within the field of mental health, which can make choosing a counselor or therapist confusing (see Question 3 for more information on the differences between a counselor, therapist, psychologist, and psychiatrist). The term "credential" can refer to the type of degree the professional has as well as the certifications and licensure they have. Although the range of credentials can include those who have obtained a bachelor's degree all the way up to a doctoral degree, the focus for this question will be on credentials that allow the professional to diagnose and treat mental illness. When choosing a counselor or therapist, some people may place a great deal of emphasis on what credentials the professional has, whereas for others the credentials are not as important as how comfortable they are with their counselor or therapist (see Question 5 for more information on how to find the right counselor or therapist). Regardless, understanding the differences between the various credentials can be helpful when identifying a counselor for one's self or a loved one.

To start with, someone who diagnoses and provides treatment for mental health issues must have an advanced degree of some kind. This means they have, at the minimum, a master's degree up to a doctoral degree. A master's degree can include an MS, MA, or MSW. The doctoral degree can include a PhD, PsyD, MD, or DNP. A master's degree usually means that the professional has two to three years of education and supervision in their specialty area (e.g., counseling, social work, psychiatric nursing) beyond the undergraduate degree. A doctoral degree can range from an additional four to eight years beyond the undergraduate degree depending on what the professional is studying. For example, a psychiatrist will have four years of education to become an MD and then another four years as a resident (practicing under supervision) in their specialty area—in this case psychiatry—before they are licensed as a psychiatrist. A psychologist usually completes four to five years of coursework and another full year as a practicing intern (during which time they practice as a psychologist would but under supervision) before they earn their PhD or PsyD. After the degree is earned, the psychologist must then practice at the minimum another full year as a psychologist while they are still under supervision before they are licensed as a psychologist and can practice independently. Thus, the primary difference between a master's degree and a doctoral degree is the amount of education and supervision the professional receives before they are licensed to practice.

In order for a professional to practice as a mental health professional who diagnoses and treats mental illness, they must obtain a license that is commensurate with their level of education and area of education. A psychiatrist must become licensed to practice as a physician. He or she may also become board certified in psychiatry although this is not required for practice. A psychologist must become licensed to practice psychology. He or she, too, may be board certified in psychology, but this is not required for practice. Professionals licensed in these two professions often do not list more than their degree after their name but may add any certifications they have below their name. For example:

Jane Smith, MD
Board Certified in Psychiatry

Licensed psychologists may list their credentials in this way:

Joe Smith, PhD
Licensed Psychologist
or
Joe Smith, PhD, LP

Other licenses may vary by state in terms of what they are called; however, most states will have a master's level counseling license that may be the licensed clinical professional counselor (LCPC) or licensed clinical social worker (LCSW). There are also licensed pastoral counselors, licensed marriage and family therapists (LMFT), and licensed psychiatric mental health nurses (PMHN), all of whom may be qualified to provide counseling or psychotherapy services. Regardless of the degrees and credentials a professional may have, it is always a good idea to talk with the professional you are considering working with, let them know what you're looking for, and ask if they can provide what you are looking for.

5. How do I find the right counselor or therapist?

Finding the right counselor or therapist may or may not be easy. The most significant issue is whether you and the counselor you are considering working with are a good fit. The catch is that you may not be able to determine that until you've had a few sessions with that professional.

It is, of course, important to determine what a counseling professional's credentials are (see Questions 3 and 4 for more information) as that may help you initially narrow down the list of possible professionals based on your personal preferences regarding the professional's level of education and training. You may also want to learn about the professional's philosophy or approach to helping people with mental health concerns. This can, of course, be found out by talking directly to the professional; however, many counselors and therapists have their own websites (or a web page if they are part of a larger organization) on which they will list their credentials and describe the services they provide. They may also include a section that describes their theoretical orientation (see Questions 7–19 to learn more about different types of therapy, which also reflect the different theoretical orientations to therapy). It can be helpful to learn some of these details about a potential counselor before talking with them as you may decide after looking at the information on their website that they do not provide the services you are looking for.

Another way to find a counselor is through word of mouth. This is often a highly reliable way to find an effective counselor. Of course, what your friend or family member liked about the counselor may not mean that you will like it too; however, you can ask them specific questions relating to what about their work with this particular counselor seemed helpful and why. Their answers may help you determine if what they are describing sounds like something you'd be looking for as well. If you ask more than one person about their counseling experiences and find that one or more names keep coming up, you have more evidence that these professionals can probably help you too.

As noted in the opening paragraph of the answer to this question, ultimately what matters most is whether you and the therapist are a good fit. This can mean any number of things but usually refers to the degree to which you feel comfortable talking with the professional and the degree to which you feel they will be helpful. The only way to truly know this is to meet with a professional at least once, but in many cases it may take a few meetings before you have a good sense of what a counseling relationship with this professional might be like for you. If, however, after the first session you feel hopeful that the professional can help and that they are listening to you and trying to understand you and your concerns, there is a good chance that this will be an effective working relationship for you.

Ultimately, what makes a counselor "right" or not has do to with what you need and whether the counselor can provide that. If you are not sure what you need, a good counselor can help you figure that out relatively quickly and then you both can determine if you will work well together.

6. I've never been to counseling before and I'm nervous about what my counselor will think about me—should I be?

Being nervous about seeing a counselor is a common experience. This is particularly the case for those who have never been to a counselor before and do not know what to expect. Even those who have seen other counselors may feel nervous about starting to work with a new counselor because of the unknown nature of a new relationship, which can include uncertainty about what this counselor might think of you and your concerns.

One of the cornerstones of effective counseling or therapy is that the professional should be nonjudgmental. This means that as you identify and describe your concerns, your thoughts, your feelings, and your actions whether in the past or present, you should feel your counselor is listening and endeavoring to understand but not judging you. This does not mean, of course, that counselors do not have opinions, thoughts, and/or reactions of their own, but they should be trained to put those aside so they can focus on you and your needs in the counseling relationship (see Question 30 for information about asking counselors direct questions). One of the ways this occurs is that counselors have a very different view of mental health and mental illness than the general population. It is common for friends, family, and strangers to wield their opinions about mental health issues in ways that can leave those struggling with their mental health feeling as if there is something wrong with them or they are weak for having such struggles. Although training varies from one professional to the next (see Questions 3 and 4 for more information about education and credentials), generally counselors learn that the causes of mental health issues are complex (e.g., genetics, culture) and that the reason one person may suffer from a mental health issue while another does not is not reflective of the quality or strength of the person but rather the nature of the mental illness and its causes.

Knowing that counselors receive specific education and training on listening and clarifying without judging may be helpful to some, but others may still worry about what their counselor thinks about their particular mental health concerns. In that case, it is perfectly acceptable to ask (see Question 30 for more information about asking questions). You can say something like "I am worried about what you must think of me," "What do you think about me and what I just said," or "All of my friends tell me I'm crazy. Do you think I'm crazy?" Your counselor's response to your direct question or statement may be all you need to feel assured that they do not think badly or negatively about you. Your question and your counselor's answer may also open up a conversation that allows you both to explore what each of you thinks and feels about mental health issues, in general, and your concerns, in particular. This can further reassure you that your counselor is truly there to help you in whatever way they can. It is possible, of course, that after having such a discussion you may not feel reassured (see Question 35 for more information about what to do if you don't like your therapist). Although this is not a good feeling, it can allow you to move on to another counselor who does leave you feeling reassured (see Question 5 for more information on finding the right counselor).

❖❖❖

Different Types of Therapy

7. What is psychoanalytic psychotherapy?

Psychoanalytic psychotherapy (a.k.a. psychoanalysis) is believed to orig-
inate with Sigmund Freud. He is considered to be the father of psychoanalysis though at the time he developed his theory many of his medical
colleagues were practicing the "talking cure." It was Freud, however, who
became an ardent student and scholar of understanding how the mind
worked and how to help people heal bruised or broken minds.

Psychoanalysis is a serious endeavor that requires a significant devo-
tion of time, effort, and money. Psychoanalysis usually takes place several
times per week (i.e., three to five times) over the course of several years.
The intent of psychoanalysis is to help each patient learn what is in their
unconscious mind so they can directly deal with those things that affect
them but about which they have been previously unaware. Freud believed
that the unconscious part of our mind was the largest and most influential
part of psychological existence. He believed that our unconscious held
not only ideas that we inherited from our biological ancestors but, more
important, our own personal desires, wishes, and urges. By developing an
understanding about or insight into this part of our mind, Freud believed
we would be able to better understand why we think, feel, and act the
way we do. The conundrum of this approach, however, is that by definition anything in our unconscious mind is inaccessible to us directly.
That is, you cannot simply think about what is in your unconscious and

then become aware of it. Freud believed the only way to gain access to the unconscious was through indirect means, such as free association, dream analysis, and slips of the tongue (a.k.a. Freudian slips). Moreover, Freud believed that there was no such thing as an accident when it comes to the experiences of human beings. Thus, even something like a slip of the tongue has an explanation and has its origins with something in the unconscious.

Another significant part of Freud's theory of psychoanalysis involves the structure of the personality. Freud believed that the personality was made up of three parts: the id, the ego, and the superego. The id operates based on the pleasure principle, which means that this is the part of our personality that wants what it wants and it wants it now (i.e., like a toddler). The superego, by contrast, operates based on the idealistic principle, meaning this part of our personality strives for perfection and is equated to our conscience. The superego does not tolerate doing things considered to be "wrong" and will scold us if we do. Finally, the ego operates based on the reality principle, which means that it tries to strike a realistic balance or compromise between the unrealistic demands of both the id and the superego. Freud believed that psychologically healthy individuals have an ego that can satisfy the demand of both id and superego. However, when the id or superego overpowers the ego, the individual will likely experience psychological problems that affect many aspects of their lives. The process of psychoanalysis is believed to help strengthen the ego.

Free association is the primary technique used in psychoanalysis. The idea behind it is simple but can be quite challenging to do in practice. Free association involves saying whatever comes to mind no matter what it is and no matter how you might feel about sharing it. The idea is to not think about it or to censure one's self but to simply say these things out loud. Once you start talking, the mind is believed to make associations between what you are saying and other memories or ideas you might not have otherwise come up with. For example, as you are saying whatever comes to mind, you may hear a train whistle outside which may remind you of another time and place that you then talk about. That time and place is likely to trigger other memories and ideas and so on. Freud believed that when free association works (i.e., when a patient is not censuring themselves), they will eventually start talking about their childhood, which is believed to be a pivotal period of time that highly influences adulthood.

Although free association is an important and effective technique in psychoanalysis, Freud believed that the "royal road" to the unconscious was dreams. As such, dream analysis is also an important tool to help both the patient and analyst understand the patient's unconscious mind. Free association is also used related to dream analysis, in that patients may be asked specifically to free-associate to different parts of their dream. The analyst will then interpret the meaning of the dream based on the analyst's understanding of the patient.

Although the analyst offers interpretations of dreams, free associations, and slips of the tongue to the patient (also referred to as the analysand), the analyst takes on what Freud referred to as the "rule of abstinence." This refers to the analyst being something like a blank slate when it comes to their interactions with and reactions to their patients. This rule means that the analyst should not offer any advice and should not show any affection for the patient. The idea is that if an analyst moves away from this kind of neutral stance the analyst risks not allowing a patient's unconscious material to surface to their conscious mind. If neurotic needs (i.e., things we do to help us feel better but that ultimately interfere with overall well-being) are gratified, such as by an analyst reassuring a patient that they are a good person worthy of being cared about or by offering advice on what the patient should do to solve a particular problem, the patient will not identify these issues as being problematic and will therefore not learn how to cope and deal with them on their own. Patients may, therefore, become dependent on the analytic relationship, which can further impede their ability to be psychologically healthy.

Another key aspect of traditional psychoanalysis involves the concept called "transference." Transference and its counterpart, "countertransference," are believed to be in play in all forms of therapy; however, transference has its roots in Freudian psychoanalysis. Transference is believed to be a reenactment of the client's Oedipal issues. In brief, Oedipal issues arise during early childhood around the age of five and involve boys falling in love with their mothers and seeing their fathers as rivals to be eliminated. The same is believed to occur for girls who fall in love with their fathers and see their mothers as rivals. If Oedipal issues are adequately resolved, then the child will learn that they cannot have the opposite-sex parent all to themselves and will begin to identify with the same-sex parent. When this occurs, boys start imitating their fathers and girls imitate their mothers. The unconscious intent is to become like their same-sex parent so that one day they can fall in love with and marry an opposite-sex partner, who is just like their opposite-sex parent (this is from where the idea of marrying someone just like your mother or father originates). When Oedipal issues are not resolved adequately, the emotions that remain tend to be pushed into the unconscious but can resurface in the form of transference. This occurs when the patient has emotional reactions to and feelings about their analyst that have nothing to do with the analyst. Those feelings have their origin in childhood and typically revolve around feelings related to the patient's mother and/or father. In psychoanalysis, transference is expected and believed to be a necessary part of effective treatment. Without experiencing transference patients cannot learn about these early, neurotic conflicts that they are unconsciously acting out on the analyst.

As previously noted, traditional Freudian psychoanalysis occurs several times a week for several years; however, many people cannot afford that kind of time and money. As such, there are what are referred to as psychoanalytically oriented therapies that use the same principles and understanding of how the mind works to help patients, but they do so one to two times per week over the course of a few months to several years. In addition, unlike traditional psychoanalysis in which the patient is lying on a couch and the analyst sits behind the patient, in psychoanalytically oriented therapies the patient and therapist sit face-to-face as is the case with other forms of therapy. Though the analyst operates in psychoanalytically oriented therapy similarly as they would in traditional psychoanalysis (e.g., take on the rule of abstinence, interpret dreams), this form of therapy is not believed to produce the same kinds of deep and pervasive changes as one would see in traditional psychoanalysis because sessions occur less frequently and usually over a shorter period of time.

8. What is psychodynamic psychotherapy?

Psychodynamic psychotherapy can be considered a close relative to psychoanalysis. In fact, in some descriptions, psychodynamic and psychoanalytic-oriented therapies are considered to be one and the same but distinct from psychoanalysis (see Question 7). Generally, however, psychodynamic psychotherapies utilize many of the same concepts and ideas that Freud believed about how the mind works.

Psychodynamic psychotherapists believe that the unconscious mind is a powerful force that significantly affects our conscious thoughts, feelings, and behaviors. In addition, it is believed that what lies in our unconscious includes experiences from our past, predominantly our childhood. Like Freud, psychodynamic psychotherapists believe that childhood experiences directly impact who we become as adults, and therefore, understanding these early experiences is key to helping adults understand and cope with their current concerns.

In addition, psychodynamic psychotherapists believe, like Freud, that all behavior is determined by something in our unconscious mind. Thus, everything we think, say out loud, feel, or do is motivated by something about which we are unaware. Every experience, therefore, is believed to be significant, worthy of understanding, and having an identifiable explanation rather than being an accident or mistake (e.g., slips of the tongue are believed to be a small window into someone's unconscious mind). Psychodynamic psychotherapists believe, like Freud, that the personality is made up of the id, ego, and superego and that psychologically healthy individuals have a strong ego that can mediate the unrealistic demands of the id and the superego (see Question 7).

Unlike traditional psychoanalysis, psychodynamic psychotherapy typically takes place once or twice per week. It is not unusual for patients to have a number of sessions similar to what they would have if they were in therapy in which the primary approach was cognitive behavioral therapy (CBT; see Question 11). Since there tend to be fewer sessions, compared to psychoanalysis, psychodynamic psychotherapy tends not to take place over the course of years; however, it can take this long depending on the needs and concerns of the patient.

Given the less frequent sessions in psychodynamic psychotherapy, another aspect of this form of therapy that can characterize the difference between this and psychanalysis has to do with how the patient's internal world is experienced or expressed. In psychanalysis the patient's internal world (both the things we're aware of and the things we are not aware of) is believed to be expressed through the relationship between the patient and the analyst (i.e., transference), whereas in psychodynamic work, the internal world of the patient is believed to be expressed through their daily lives and what's going on around them. Thus, although psychodynamic psychotherapists acknowledge that transference can occur (see Question 7), it is not believed to be a critical part of the treatment process since transference has less of an opportunity to develop and intensify as it would with psychoanalysis.

When push comes to shove, psychodynamic psychotherapy has similar aims as psychoanalysis. Both approaches take the position that the unconscious is pivotal in understanding someone and that becoming aware of our unconscious motives (i.e., insight) is important for effective treatment. Both approaches also believe that early childhood experiences are critical to understanding who an adult is. Ultimately practitioners of either approach believe that the unconscious mind holds the answers to questions such as why a patient may simultaneously seem to want to change and not want to change despite whatever pain they may be experiencing.

9. What is behavior therapy?

Behavior therapy takes the approach that any behavior—which includes what we do, what we think, and how we feel—was learned in one way or another. This includes behaviors that are undesirable or are symptoms of a mental illness. The idea is that since any behavior is learned any behavior can be unlearned. From this perspective, understanding one's behaviors means that one must understand major theories of learning that include classical conditioning, operant conditioning, and observational learning.

Those familiar with classical conditioning may recall hearing about an experiment conducted by Russian physiologist Ivan Pavlov. The experiment is often referred to as Pavlov's dogs experiment, which involved dogs salivating at the sound of a bell. As a physiologist Pavlov was originally interested in developing a greater understanding of how animal bodies worked. As such, he was in the process of studying the digestive behavior of dogs by placing meat powder in front of them and collecting the saliva they produced as a result of smelling the meat powder. By accident, Pavlov discovered that the dogs had learned when they were about to get the meat powder and began salivating *before* the meat powder was given to them. This made Pavlov wonder if dogs could be trained to start salivating to any stimulus that was associated with food. This observation and question led him to develop the experiment widely known today.

Pavlov rang a bell just before giving the dog some meat powder. Initially the bell had no effect on the dog (which would be expected), at least not in terms of salivation. He did this several times—rang a bell and then gave the dog meat powder—until the dog began salivating at the sound of the bell. When this happened, he concluded the dog had learned that the bell was an indicator of what the dog really wanted and was about to be presented. Thus, the dog made the connection between the bell and the meat powder. Pavlov and others experimented further to determine what conditions produced the fastest learning, such as whether stimuli different from but similar to the original stimulus would produce the same results. Pavlov's original experiment lead to our understanding that all animals (including human beings) can learn in this way. Think about it like this. When there are dark clouds outside along with rain and you see a bright flash of light, most people know what is coming next—thunder. Some people count the seconds, some people cover their ears, and others brace themselves for the loud sound. Either way, we have learned through classical conditioning that lightning is followed by thunder. Without thunder, we generally would not give too much thought to lightning (unless, of course, you are near the lightning strike itself). Another example, found with pets, involves any routine you have that results in the pet getting something it really wants, like food or going outside for a walk. The sound of the can opener or rustle of the bag of food means nothing to your pet until it connects that sound with the presence of food. Then, the pet gets excited the moment it hears the sound. Likewise, if you always put on your sneakers or always shake your keys before you take your dog for a walk, your dog will get excited by the sound of the keys or the fact that you're putting on your sneakers—not because that is so exciting but because the dog has learned that those events come right before what they really want, which is to go for a walk.

Classical conditioning has been used to explain how some fears or phobias develop. For example, if you had a bad experience with a dog in a park (the dog growled and barked loudly at you and was only stopped by its owner holding the leash) and if this experience was powerful enough, you may now associate the park with the aggressive dog and feel apprehensive or fearful when at the park even when dogs are not around. Behavioral therapists using the principles of classical conditioning to treat this kind of fear will help the patient learn to associate other more positive experiences with being in the park so that the patient can learn that being at the park is enjoyable or, at the very least, not scary.

Another form of learning, operant conditioning, involves understanding the consequences of your behaviors in the form of a reward or punishment. The idea behind this form of learning is simple: the more a behavior is rewarded, the more likely a person or animal will engage in that behavior again, and the more a behavior is punished, the less likely a person or animal will engage in that behavior again. For example, if you tell a joke and people laugh at the joke, you are more likely to tell that joke or other jokes again. If people do not laugh at your jokes, then you might be less likely to tell jokes in the future. Similarly, the paycheck you receive is intended to reward you for the good work you do and so you will keep doing it, and the ticket you get from speeding is intended to punish you for going too fast so that you don't speed anymore. My guess is that some readers may have already found the flaw in this theory. A ticket does not always prevent someone from speeding again, and a paycheck may not be enough to keep someone from doing good work. Thus, when rewards and punishments are used to shape behavior, it is important to use rewards and punishments that feel rewarding or punishing to the person receiving that consequence. A child, for example, that throws tantrums and gets yelled at by a parent may or may not stop having tantrums. It all depends on whether the attention the child just got from the parent was rewarding (e.g., this is the only attention they ever get) or punishing (e.g., they really don't like being yelled at by their parent). Whatever the child does afterward tells the parents whether what they did was rewarding or punishing. If the child keeps throwing tantrums, either the child was rewarded, or at the very least the yelling was not much of a punishment. If the child stops throwing tantrums, then it is likely that the yelling was experienced as a punishment.

In a variety of treatment models, rewards are often used to reinforce good behavior and undesired behavior is often ignored. For example, in a group home where adolescents with behavioral problems live until they are ready to return home, they may receive tokens or points for good behavior that they can then trade in for rewards, such as a treat or time spent at home. Similarly, they may lose tokens or points when they engage in undesired behavior, making their ability to earn rewards more difficult.

The final learning theory, observational learning, involves what it implies—we learn by observing others. We see the behaviors others engage in as well as what consequences they receive as a result of that behavior. We then learn to engage in some behaviors and avoid others simply by watching what happens to other people. What is important with this theory of learning has to do with who we are observing. The person from whom we are vicariously learning has to be important to us in one way or another. Often this is a sibling, peer, parent, or other role model. Role models can be anyone we know and admire or look up to, such as a coach or a peer who is older than us or those we don't know but admire and look up to anyway like a celebrity. The choice of a role model is important, particularly when it comes to celebrities who seem to "get away with" a lot of "bad" behavior. This can teach those who look up to a particular role model that if the role model does a socially undesirable behavior (e.g., break the law, behave badly) but does not get punished for it, that can lead those who look up to that role model to emulate the role model's behavior because they believe it is okay.

Elements of each of these theories of learning can be used to help people learn new, desired behaviors and to unlearn old, undesired behaviors.

One of these most well-known and heavily researched treatment methods that uses principles of learning is called systematic desensitization. This treatment method is used to help people who have phobias. Phobias are defined as an unreasonable fear of an object (e.g., spiders) or situation (e.g., heights). Systematic desensitization uses principles of classical conditioning to help the person unlearn the fear that is associated with their phobia and to learn to be calm when dealing with their fear. It works by the therapist and patient working together to develop a fear hierarchy. This means that they identify up to 10 versions of the feared object or situation that result in a range of reactions from causing some discomfort up to intense fear. For example, someone with a fear of spiders may have as their lowest item on the fear hierarchy the word "spider." The next item might be seeing a cartoon drawing of a spider, then a realistic drawing of a spider, and so on until the person got to the highest item on the hierarchy which might involve being near a spider that is not contained in anyway (i.e., it is not in a cage/tank or under a glass). Often the patient is also taught a form of relaxation they can use when going through their fear hierarchy, although recent research has indicated that intentionally engaging in relaxation may hinder the treatment process as the person needs to experience the fear to realize that they can survive it. Relaxation, then, would only be used if the person has such an intense fear reaction that they need to use relaxation to avoid hyperventilating or having a panic attack.

10. What is cognitive therapy?

Cognitive therapy is based on the idea that all of our experiences, thoughts, feelings, and behaviors are interconnected. When we experience symptoms of a disorder or simply identify aspects of ourselves we'd like to change, a cognitive therapist will focus on specific thoughts we have as well as, but to a lesser degree, our feelings and behaviors.

Primarily, cognitive therapy focuses on inaccurate and irrational thought processes. The idea is that by identifying such beliefs and changing them to something more productive or rational an individual's emotional experiences will also change along with any behaviors that may have resulted from irrational beliefs. Thus, although feelings and behaviors matter to a cognitive therapist, they will direct their efforts to the thoughts someone is having since problematic thoughts lead to problematic feelings and behaviors and, thus, changing thoughts will be followed by a change in emotions and behaviors.

Work in the area of cognitive therapy began as early as the 1950s with psychologist Albert Ellis. He originally called his approach *rational therapy*, which was later named *rational emotive therapy* and then finally *rational emotive behavior therapy* (this is a precursor to what is now known as cognitive behavioral therapy [CBT; see Question 11]). In the 1960s psychologist Aaron Beck established cognitive therapy as a viable mode of treatment for psychological distress and later formalized his approach as CBT.

The cognitive approaches were developed, in part, as a response to the previously dominant approaches: psychoanalytic and psychodynamic psychotherapies (see Questions 7 and 8, respectively). Those focusing more on cognitions (i.e., the ways in which a person perceives and understands their daily experiences) did not agree with the traditional Freudian approach of helping patients gain insight into what is going on with them unconsciously. Similarly, focusing on cognitions was at odds with behavioral approaches to treatment (see Question 9), which took the position that a focus on "mental" (i.e., cognitive) causes of behavior was unscientific and therefore not useful compared to the highly structured and scientific approach of identifying specific behaviors that could be easily identified and then changed through the use of principles of learning. By the 1970s, however, cognitive approaches to treatment had a solid footing in the study of mental health and treatment of diagnosable issues.

Overall, cognitive therapies involve challenging the thoughts a patient may have about themselves, which are often negative. The challenge takes the form of reality testing by identifying negative thoughts or beliefs and asking the patient for evidence that those beliefs are true while other, more rational, beliefs are not. While it is typically the case a patient can find evidence that supports the gist of their maladaptive thought or belief, oftentimes the maladaptive thoughts are in the form of an absolute. For example, someone may make a mistake and think "I'm so stupid, I can't do this" or "I'm not good at anything." These thoughts are likely to lead to negative emotions (e.g., feeling frustrated, sad, or angry), which may then lead to maladaptive behaviors such as giving up on things that present as even a little bit challenging or not starting new challenges to begin with. The second thought is usually easier to refute than the first as it is highly unlikely that someone is truly not good at anything; however, both are declarative statements that make no room for any alternative perspective. The cognitive therapist will challenge the patient to practice more flexible ways of thinking. For example, instead of thinking "I'm so stupid, I can't do this," the therapist may suggest thinking something like

"This is really difficult for me and I am struggling to get this done right now." This thought allows room for the idea that whatever is challenging or difficult now may not always be so and that the person may simply need a break from the task or to approach it from another perspective. Regardless, the task is to help the patient refute ways of thinking that are harmful and replace them with ways of thinking that are more realistic and allow for other possibilities that the patient has not thought of.

Ultimately the skills learned in therapy using this approach are intended to be used by the patient in the real world and not just in the therapist's office. In this way the patient learns to be their own therapist, identifying problematic ways of thinking that lead to negative feelings and maladaptive behaviors. Cognitive therapy is usually a short-term form of therapy and may be designed so that a patient meets with the therapist once a week for six to eight weeks. This means that the sole focus of the work is on current, problematic cognitions and helping the patient recognize them when they occur and changing them to more productive ways of thinking.

11. What is cognitive behavioral therapy (CBT)?

Cognitive behavioral therapy (CBT) is the form of treatment that many people have previously heard of. It has been studied more than any other form of therapy in large part because the elements of the approach are easy to identify and easy to measure (both of which are important when conducting a scientific study). The unconscious, for example, which is important in the psychoanalytic and psychodynamic treatments (see Questions 7 and 8, respectively), is exceedingly difficult to identify and measure, which means it is difficult at best, if not impossible, to accurately measure. Thus, much less research has been conducted on the elements of these forms of therapy. CBT can be done or delivered in a variety of ways, but all approaches will focus on the thoughts and behaviors that cause someone distress and help alleviate that distress via solutions designed to target specific problems.

Although CBT includes both "cognitive" and "behavior" in its name, its roots are grounded in cognitive therapy (see Question 10) more so than behavior therapy (see Question 9). CBT is considered to be a problem- or solution-focused form of psychotherapy. By contrast, historical approaches such as psychoanalytic and psychodynamic psychotherapy sought to help patients understand their problems, which would lead to helpful changes in them and their lives, but the focus was not on identifying a specific problem and a specific solution for that problem (e.g., a mental health diagnosis such as major depressive disorder). Thus, the ultimate goal of CBT is to identify effective strategies designed to eliminate the symptoms of a particular disorder.

As is the case with cognitive therapy, CBT focuses on problematic thinking patterns that, in turn, negatively impact behavior and emotions. The primary focus is on cognitive distortions, which refer to ways of thinking that are inaccurate and, in some cases, are flat out wrong. Cognitive distortions include overgeneralizing (e.g., I am bad at this so I am bad at everything), magnifying negatives (i.e., only seeing or remembering what went wrong or what was bad and ignoring or forgetting about what went right or what was good), minimizing positives (i.e., acknowledging good things but downplaying them as not that important), and catastrophizing (i.e., imagining the worst-case scenario and believing that is what will happen). CBT helps patients identify their cognitive distortions and replace them with thoughts and beliefs that are more realistic and grounded in reality. Doing so is believed to help reduce emotional distress and decrease behaviors that are self-sabotaging.

With regard to the behavioral element of CBT, patients may experience something called exposure and skills training. "Exposure" refers to exposing the patient to situations (e.g., riding in an elevator) or things (e.g., snakes) that they fear or are uncomfortable with and tend to avoid. The idea is that when we avoid situations or things we're afraid of, we reinforce the notion that what we're avoiding is something that we should feel afraid of. For example, if you are fearful of giving a speech in front of the class, then skip class the day you are supposed to give your speech; you temporarily feel better, which can lead you to conclude that since you feel better because you avoided it, it is, in fact, something you should be afraid of. Thus, a part of CBT involves working with the patient to expose themselves to what they fear. Skills training involves teaching patients strategies they can use in their everyday lives to help them effectively cope with things that normally cause them distress. For example, a patient may be taught a brief relaxation script they can use when they start to feel anxious about something, or how to identify and challenge maladaptive thoughts they routinely have.

CBT has been found to be an effective form of treatment for a variety of mental illnesses. For example, when compared to medication, CBT has been shown to be at least as effective in reducing symptoms for many (though not all) disorders as medication. It is, therefore, often recommended that with more severe disorders CBT in combination with medication is an effective approach to treatment. Since CBT is fairly straightforward in practice, it has been adapted for use outside of the traditional therapy setting and can be used via the Internet and self-help manuals and in psychoeducational or skills training groups.

12. What is supportive psychotherapy?

Supportive psychotherapy has its roots tied to psychoanalytic psychotherapy (see Question 7), in that supportive psychotherapy was historically offered as the "not psychoanalysis" form of treatment. Psychoanalysis and other similar forms of psychotherapy require that patients be able to self-reflect and hear and use the interpretations offered by the psychoanalyst. When patients were unable, for whatever reason, to do what is required for psychoanalysis, then supportive psychotherapy was offered. Since then, however, supportive psychotherapy has emerged as a form of treatment that is not what is left when nothing else works but a bona fide treatment method that has been shown in research to be as effective as other forms of psychotherapy. Some have suggested that it should be the treatment of choice for many, if not most, patients.

Defining supportive psychotherapy is not quite as clear cut as it is to define other forms of psychotherapy. Nonetheless, this form of treatment can be defined as a method used to help patients cope with emotional distress and the difficulties patients have in managing and enjoying their daily lives. Some of the primary strategies used by supportive psychotherapists come from cognitive behavioral therapy (see Question 11), client-centered or Rogerian psychotherapy (see Question 14), and interpersonal psychotherapy (see Question 13). Some readers familiar with the concept of eclectic therapy (see Question 15) may think supportive psychotherapy is a type of eclectic psychotherapy. It is not. Despite the fact that strategies and techniques used in this approach are gleaned from a variety of approaches, the fact of the matter is that supportive psychotherapy is a form of treatment in and of itself. Supportive psychotherapy prizes the therapeutic alliance—the connection that exists between the patient and his or her counselor—and is focused on helping the patient feel effective in their life and to feel good about themselves. What follows is a brief description of some of the techniques used in this form of treatment.

"Praise" can and should be used throughout a session and throughout the course of treatment. This is not praise for praise's sake but is an opportunity for the therapist to overtly recognize progress made or things the patient has done well. As is the case in any interaction, praise is effective only when it is offered sincerely and accurately. That is, the therapist has to mean it, and the therapist needs to praise something that is deserving of praise. For example, saying something like "Good job showing up on time today" will land like a ton of bricks for a patient who has no trouble with this, but it may be an invaluable comment for another patient who wants to improve their punctuality and has struggled to show up on time for sessions and other important appointments. What would likely follow such a comment is something like "What do you think allowed you to be punctual today?" This will help the patient become aware of and reinforce skills they implemented that are new to them or that they hadn't realized they were using.

"Reassurance," like praise, should be offered only when it can be done so genuinely. It should not feel to the patient as though they are being patronized. Moreover, when offered, the patient ought to feel as though the therapist is reassuring them based on what the therapist knows about the patient. That is, the reassurance should feel as though it is offered specifically for that patient based on what that patient needs at that time. Therapists, for example, can reassure patients concerned about whether therapy will help them that it is effective for their particular concerns and that it will help the patient feel better. It would not, however, make sense to reassure a patient in this way if they have utilized therapy throughout their life with success; they already know therapy will be effective for them.

The technique of "normalizing" is a specific type of reassurance that takes on the form of letting the patient know they are not alone with their struggles—that their concerns are similar to or the same as what a lot of people experience. Sometimes patients are helped by reassurance that involves letting them know that their experiences do not make them "crazy" and that what they are experiencing is common. This can be tricky, however, if the patient's concerns are normalized in such a way that they feel like their unique situation is not fully understood. Normalizing used in this way can feel to the patients as though their concerns have been trivialized or dismissed as not that big of a deal—when to the patients themselves it is a big deal.

"Encouragement" can be used with all patients with any type or severity of concern. Higher-functioning patients can be encouraged to reach for realistic goals that they have previously not worked toward or have talked themselves out of. They can be encouraged to make a plan that allows them to take reasonable steps toward such goals. Patients who struggle such that they find it difficult to take care of daily tasks and to engage in self-care can be encouraged to keep attending their appointments and to develop skills that will help them lead a healthier, more satisfying life.

"Reframing" is a technique that involves helping a patient see an element of their experience from a different perspective. Reframing has occurred when someone says "I hadn't thought of it that way before." A statement like this means that someone else has offered an explanation for or a perspective on the other person's situation that they do not likely have themselves. For example, problems a patient may be experiencing can be reframed as opportunities to try something new, or a perceived weakness may be reframed as a strength. Like other techniques, reframing ought not to be used just because it can be. Rather, it should be used when the therapist sees an opportunity to help a patient see something from a different perspective when the patient's current perspective does not seem to be serving them well.

"Advice" and "teaching" are two additional techniques used by supportive psychotherapists. Offering advice is often something that students of counseling and psychotherapy are taught early on that they should, at the very least, be wary of, if not avoid altogether. The danger of giving advice lies with the possibility that the patient may come to rely on the therapist for what to do rather than building the skills themselves. Nonetheless, advice, when considered carefully, can be offered in ways that are ultimately beneficial for patients and for the development of new skills. Advice is best offered when it is clear that the direction provided is connected to the patient's goals. For example, a patient who came to therapy for help with a dating relationship may receive the following advice from their therapist: "We've been working together for several weeks and each time you talk about your partner you end up crying because of how your partner treats you. I am worried, too, about how you are being treated and think it may be time to consider ending the relationship." When the therapist uses the related technique of teaching, they are taking the step of helping the patient learn more about themselves and how to make effective and healthy decisions. For example, a therapist might recognize that their patient is an introvert and that this personality trait may help explain how and why the patient struggles in their current relationships. As such, the therapist may offer information about introversion, what it is, how it affects interactions with others, and so on. The therapist may also recommend a book or trusted website for the patient to read more about a particular topic.

13. What is interpersonal psychotherapy?

Interpersonal psychotherapy, as the name suggests, focuses on the patient's interpersonal relationships. The nature of a patient's interpersonal relationships, according to this approach, is believed to be the cause of and maintaining factor in a patient's distress. The goal of this form of treatment is to reduce symptoms and to see overall improvement in one's interpersonal relationships, including an increase in social support.

Interpersonal psychotherapy was originally developed at Yale University in the 1970s, particularly as a method of treatment for depression. It has since been studied and applied to myriad other disorders such as bulimia nervosa, bipolar disorder, and postpartum depression. The treatment itself is time-limited, which means it is designed to be brief. This usually means that a patient will work with a therapist once a week for approximately 12–16 weeks, and there is a distinct beginning, middle, and an end. In the beginning of treatment (approximately three sessions), the task is to identify what the mental health diagnosis is and the nature of interpersonal interactions when the symptoms are usually evident. The middle phase of this form of treatment involves the therapist working with the patient on the nature of the interpersonal issues that seem to contribute to the patient's current distress. The final phase of treatment is important, in that the therapist emphasizes the fact that treatment will be coming to an end while simultaneously bolstering the patient's skills and abilities so the patient feels more capable of handling their concerns on their own. The nature of time-limited therapy and the reminder that the therapy has an ending put pressure on the patient to take action. Although the nature of the relationship between the therapist and patient is important, the focus remains on the patient's relationships and situation outside of the therapeutic environment. The primary theories that underlie this approach are attachment theory and communication theory.

Attachment theory comes from the field of developmental psychology and states that the physical and emotional connections, or bond, a child has with at least one primary caretaker (i.e., whoever is raising the child) is necessary for optimal development. This type of bond allows the developing child to feel like the world is a safe and stable place, and this person serves as a "home base" from which the child can express their individuality, grow, and take risks. Communication theory takes the perspective that we all communicate in one form or another (e.g., through our words, tone of voice, body language). From the perspective of psychology, this theory involves extending our understanding of communication to include the thoughts and feelings of the person doing the communication. In this theory there is a sender and a receiver of communication, and in order to function effectively, it is important for us to be able to effectively communicate with one another as both a sender of a message and a receiver of a message. Thus, both the ability to attach to someone early in life and the ability to communicate effectively with others are critical components of our interpersonal relationships and thus to the process of interpersonal psychotherapy.

Although the quality of the relationship between the patient and therapist is believed to be a critical factor in the effectiveness of treatment for other forms of psychotherapy (e.g., see Questions 7 and 14), it makes a great deal of sense why this would also be an important factor for interpersonal psychotherapy. Since the nature of one's relationships with others is believed to be a contributing factor to people's distress, it would follow that the patient–therapist relationship ought to yield important information to help with understanding and ultimately resolving the patient's distress. This approach also uses the "diathesis-stress model" to understand psychological problems. This means that someone has to have the genetics (diathesis) for a particular problem in order for it to develop *and* the right kind of environment (stress) that will trigger the problem to develop or emerge. Without either, according to this model, the problem will not develop to begin with. The primary stress from the perspective of interpersonal psychotherapy is interpersonal distress. Thus, whatever mental health concerns someone is experiencing, they have to have the genetics for that particular problem to develop (e.g., anxiety, depression, an eating disorder), and they have to have the kind of interpersonal relationships that would trigger that concern to develop. To more fully explain why someone may be in distress, the interpersonal psychotherapy approach to mental health concerns uses the "interpersonal triad" as a more complete explanation. The triad involves (1) an acute interpersonal crisis, (2) insufficient social support, and (3) the nature of one's attachment, genetics, culture, spirituality, personal vulnerabilities, and personal strengths.

Some techniques used in this approach include role-playing (i.e., the therapist plays the role of someone in the patient's life and they role-play how a specific conversation might go), communication analysis in which the patient provides details about a specific conversation with a focus on how the patient felt and what they intended to communicate, and use of content and process affect which refers to understanding what emotions the patient feels or has felt (in an interpersonal interaction) and their understanding of these emotions (e.g., what they mean, why they occurred).

14. What is client-centered therapy?

Client-centered therapy is also referred to as person-centered therapy. The name change reflects the developer's recognition that the principles that apply to helping clients in psychotherapy also apply to people in general and our interactions with others.

Client-centered therapy was developed by psychologist Carl Rogers in the 1940s; however, his paper published in 1959 entitled "The Necessary and Sufficient Conditions of Therapeutic Personality Change" is believed to be among the most important, if not the most important, contribution to the establishment of this approach. In this paper he describes six specific conditions that, if met, are the *only* conditions necessary in therapy for meaningful change to occur. The six conditions are as follows: (1) there must be a client who is experiencing distress and needs assistance in some way, (2) the client and therapist meet regularly over a period of time, (3) the therapist is congruent, (4) the therapist can express unconditional positive regard for the client, (5) the therapist is able to be empathic with the client and his or her experiences, and (6) the client experiences the therapist as being congruent, as having unconditional positive regard, and as being empathic.

Conditions 3–5 fall under the purview of the therapist, meaning it is the therapist's job to make sure he or she is able to interact with the client in these ways. Condition 3, congruence, is a term that effectively refers to genuineness. This means that if the therapist is congruent or genuine, he or she is being true to who they are and that what the therapist says or does reflects what they actually are thinking or feeling. When this occurs the client will experience the therapist as being "real" and that the therapist is sincere and honest. Condition 4, unconditional positive regard, is a term that refers to the degree to which the therapist can accept the client as they are. This is the condition that reflects the idea that the therapist is able to interact with a client without judgment. Thus, if a client reveals something about themselves they fear may be criticized, a therapist who has unconditional positive regard for or acceptance of the client will not judge or criticize the client in any way. Condition 5, empathy, is a concept that is often confused with sympathy. Sympathy refers to feeling, for example, badly for someone based on what the other person has experienced (e.g., the death of a loved one). Empathy, on the other hand, refers to being able to know what the other person is feeling at a deeper level than what the client may have expressed. For example, a client may say that he or she is feeling really sad about an important loss and is crying inconsolably. The therapist may say something like "This loss is devastating for you and is, perhaps, the worst type of loss you could experience." A statement such as this characterizes the loss as something more significant than something the client feels "sad" about. Clearly, the client is sad, but their experience is more profound than that.

These three conditions, as noted, are critical for the therapist to be able to do; however, what is equally, if not more, critical is whether the client perceives the therapist as congruent (genuine), as having unconditional positive regard (acceptance), and as empathic (Condition 6). If the client does not perceive the therapist in these ways, then those three conditions have not been met and psychotherapy is not going to be effective. For example, if the therapist believes he or she truly is genuine, accepting, and empathic but the client feels there is something "fake" about the therapist and/or the client feels like the therapist might be secretly judging them and/or the client does not agree with the therapist's empathic statement (e.g., "No, the loss isn't quite that bad"), then it is as if those three things have not occurred, and as a result therapy will not be effective.

In order to convey genuineness, acceptance, and empathy, a client-centered therapist will use techniques such as active listening, summarizing, and asking open-ended questions. Techniques such as these are used in the spirit of following the client's lead (the therapist does not determine what is talked about in therapy), of trying to fully understand the client from his or her perspective, and of fostering an atmosphere of curiosity and self-exploration so the client can make decisions that are best for him or her rather than the therapist giving advice on what the client could or should do.

When the therapist is successful in conveying genuineness, acceptance, and empathy in such a way that the client experiences those things, Rogers believed that the client would undergo a process of increasingly sharing more of themselves resulting in an irreversible, positive change. Rogers stated that initially in therapy a client is likely to be guarded or defensive and may be cautious about sharing meaningful and emotional experiences. As therapy progresses under the six conditions noted previously, clients will eventually start sharing more of their internal and highly emotional experiences—much of which may be things that when shared with others have been criticized, judged, or dismissed as not that important. When the therapist gives the client a different experience (i.e., the therapist genuinely accepts the client as is regardless of what is shared and can empathize with the client's emotions), the client will begin to share more and will allow into their own awareness things they may have tried to keep hidden from themselves. For example, a client may say, "I hadn't realized this before, but I really cannot stand the profession I've chosen. I've convinced myself it is great and that I love it, but really I can't stand it and I think that is why I feel depressed/anxious/irritable a lot of the time." Rogers would say that the only reason the client became aware of this reality and was willing to share it with the therapist was all six of the previously mentioned conditions had been met. Without them the client would not have learned about this important reality.

As the client more freely allows into their own awareness things about themselves that they had previously denied (e.g., "I don't hate my career"; "I haven't fallen out of love with my partner and we are not beyond repair") or distorted (e.g., "My career is not *that* bad"; "My relationship with my partner is not great but I think it is fixable"), they will, themselves, become more congruent or genuine. That is, a client's expressed thoughts, feelings, and behaviors will accurately reflect what they are truly experiencing internally. When the client feels sad, they will say so or display sadness in some way. When the client feels angry, they will recognize it and figure out how to express their anger and appropriately do something about what has made them angry. The client will also become more accepting of themselves as they are, flaws and all. The client will no longer strive to become an "ideal" often unattainable version of themselves that typically has little, if any, room for imperfection. The client will also experience less tension overall (both physically and psychologically), and their relationships will improve. Sometimes part of this type of improvement may include ending relationships that the client now honestly recognizes as being harmful to them. Finally, clients who undergo psychotherapy when all six conditions are met will be more accepting of themselves and other people. That is, they will take on the perspective of unconditional positive regard for themselves and others. This occurs, in large part, because they have recognized that they are not perfect, that they make mistakes, *and* that they are still a person worthy of love and acceptance. When they can do this, then other people's flaws or mistakes are seen in the same light.

15. What is eclectic therapy?

Therapy or counseling approaches that use concepts and techniques from more than one "pure" form of therapy (e.g., cognitive behavioral therapy [see Question 11], psychoanalytic psychotherapy [see Question 7]) can be referred to as eclectic psychotherapy, synthetic psychotherapy, or integrative psychotherapy. Eclectic psychotherapy means that the therapist will select techniques with which they are familiar to use as needed based on the client's needs. Synthetic psychotherapy means that both techniques (e.g., using dream analysis to understand the unconscious mind; using systematic desensitization for treating a phobia) and theoretical concepts (e.g., understanding the unconscious is critical for effective psychotherapy; all behaviors are learned and therefore can be unlearned) are combined to help clients. Integrative psychotherapy uses elements of various treatment approaches that are combined under a system of psychotherapy. That is, specific theoretical concepts and techniques are drawn from other pure forms of therapy and combined in such a way that they form a new therapeutic approach to helping clients—all clients are treated using this combination of ideas.

The differences between these three approaches are subtle; however, the overriding similarity is that all three use techniques and theoretical concepts from more than one approach to help clients. The idea is that all pure forms of therapy have merit (see Questions 18 and 19), and by selecting ideas and skills from more than one approach, either on a case-by-case basis or in a more formalized way, therapists will more effectively meet the wide variety of needs that clients present. Another supposition of those who combine approaches is that *common factors* are believed to be the reason why change occurs in the pure forms of therapy. Thus, it is not so much the specific approach used but these other underlying factors that are important (see Question 19). Truly eclectic psychotherapy cannot be described more specifically since the techniques and ideas used will vary based on what the client needs and based on the knowledge and training of the therapist. For example, a therapist without education or training in psychoanalytic (see Question 7) or psychodynamic psychotherapy (see Question 8) will not use anything from those approaches, whereas an eclectic therapist who has may use ideas and skills from those approaches if they fit the clients' needs.

As previously noted, any approach that systematically combines skills and ideas from more than one approach would be considered a form of integrative psychotherapy; however, integrated psychotherapies have also been considered forms of eclectic psychotherapy. Some of those models include multimodal therapy developed by Arnold Lazarus, systematic eclectic psychotherapy developed by Larry Beutler, functional eclectic therapy developed by Joseph Hart, transtheoretical approach developed by James Prochaska, eclectic approach developed by Sol Garfield, pragmatic therapy developed by Richard Discoll, and integrated psychotherapy developed by Ferdinand Knobloch and Jirina Knobloch. Describing each of these approaches is beyond the scope of this book; however, Prochaska's transtheoretical approach is among those that have been heavily researched and is still in use today as well as in a variety of contexts outside the therapy or counseling setting.

The primary idea underlying the transtheoretical approach is the degree to which clients are ready to make changes. As such, this approach uses the "stages of change," which includes precontemplation, contemplation, preparation, action, and maintenance. The precontemplation stage is considered the "not yet ready" stage. In this stage a client is likely to reject, outright, the idea of making a change. In the contemplation stage, often referred to as the "getting ready" stage, a client likely acknowledges that change may be needed but is not quite ready to take steps to make any changes. In the preparation stage clients are considered "ready" for change and are probably working on a plan to make needed changes. During the action stage clients enact their plan to actually make the changes they want to make, and the maintenance stage refers to the time when clients take action to ensure the changes they've made will last. Although in many cases people progress through these stages in a stepwise, linear manner, it is also possible for people to "jump around" the stages and start with, for example, precontemplation and then seemingly jump to preparation only to go back to precontemplation.

An element that helps to predict or identify where in the stages of change a client may be involves a decision-making process that is understood in terms of pros and cons. For example, when a client is in the precontemplation stage, the pros for making change are outweighed by the cons for making change, and when in the contemplation stage, when clients are not quite ready for change, they may seem ambivalent about making change because they can see equal value in the pros and the cons for making change. When the balance sheet of pros and cons changes such that the pros for making change outweigh the cons, then the client is likely ready to take action (preparation stage) or may dive right into taking action (action stage).

Another important factor involved in understanding a client and their desire to make change has to do with the concept of self-efficacy. Self-efficacy refers to whether a client believes they can make changes to begin with or to maintain the changes they have made, particularly when they are in situations that might result in a relapse. A client, for example, who is dealing with alcoholism may not believe they can stop drinking. This means the client has low self-efficacy for making behavior changes and is probably in the precontemplation stage of change. Alternatively, a client who is dealing with alcoholism and has worked hard to change their drinking habits may doubt their ability to not drink when they are surrounded by friends who do drink or during holidays when gatherings may involve alcohol. In this case, the client is in a later stage of change but has low self-efficacy with respect to their ability to resist temptation or to say no to invitations where they know alcohol will be available. Understanding a client's level of self-efficacy at any stage in the behavior change process does not necessarily predict the outcome but can help both client and therapist understand why behavior change or maintenance is challenging or not going as planned.

Finally, the transtheoretical approach states that there are specific processes that must occur for behavior change to take place, and these processes help explain how change occurs in clients. These processes of change are categorized in terms of whether the process in question is cognitive (e.g., thoughts, ideas) or affective (i.e., emotions) or behavioral. Cognitive and affective processes are identified as consciousness raising, dramatic relief, environmental reevaluation, self-reevaluation, and social liberation. Behavioral processes include self-liberation, counterconditioning, helping relationships, reinforcement management, and stimulus control. Many of these elements reflect concepts from cognitive therapy (see Question 10), behavior therapy (see Question 9), or cognitive behavioral therapy (see Question 11).

Overall those who practice using the transtheoretical approach understand that change takes time and people require assistance and support as they go about making behavior change. Helping clients make behavior change can be aided by maximizing the pros for change and minimizing the cons. Many people who are considered to be *at risk* will not be ready or prepared to take action on the changes they would like to make; therefore, helping people get to a stage closer to taking action should be the goal rather than taking action itself. Finally, the principles and processes that underlie this approach must be identified and reinforced throughout the change process in order for progress to occur.

16. What is group therapy?

Group therapy is different from individual counseling and therapy but is an equally valid and important form of treatment. It is different from individual forms of treatment in terms of how many people are involved, how long a meeting may last, and the benefits and drawbacks to group therapy that may make this mode of treatment more or less valuable to a particular patient.

Generally, group therapy involves a group of around 10 patients (range is usually 5–15 clients), who have some shared concern or interest, and the group sessions are facilitated by one or two therapists. Meetings can be scheduled for one to two hours, and each meeting may serve a particular purpose or the approach to therapy may be to allow things to flow out of whatever the members bring up during the session. A group may be formed based on diagnosis (e.g., group for people who are depressed, anxious, or have an eating disorder). When the group is formed based on a diagnosis, the understanding is that the focus will be on helping group members with shared symptoms associated with that disorder. Sometimes a group may be formed based on a shared concern such as "relationship issues" or "divorce" or some other issue that is not necessarily diagnosable but that is interfering with group members' overall well-being. Still other groups may be formed based on building specific skills such as effective communication and parenting skills. In this instance, there is not a shared diagnosis but a shared desire to learn about or improve on a particular skill from which many people can benefit.

Just as individual psychotherapy can take many different approaches to working on the concern of a patient (e.g., psychoanalytic, person centered; see Questions 7–15), so too can group therapy. Thus, the group may involve psychoanalytic group therapy, cognitive behavioral group therapy, client-centered group therapy, and so on. The therapeutic approach of the group therapy will be determined, in large part, by the therapist(s)' training and to a lesser extent by the reason the group members have come together (e.g., based on diagnosis, skill building). As noted previously, the value that group therapy brings for a client may be different than the value they may get from individual therapy. There are many experiences that can occur in group therapy that do not necessarily occur in individual therapy. A discussion of some of those benefits follows.

One of the major reasons why clients indicate they benefit from and/ or like group therapy is the sense of universality the group brings. This means that they are not alone with their concerns; rather, they are interacting with many others who understand their experiences in a way that most others do not. Benefits of knowing they are not alone with their concerns can include an increase in self-esteem, validation of what they experience, and a decrease in a sense of isolation. Another benefit to group therapy that is not likely to occur in individual therapy is the notion that as a member of a group each client has an opportunity to learn from and assist one another. In individual therapy the assumption and expectation is that the therapist will help the client, not vice versa. This is certainly useful, and many clients prefer this; however, in a group, experiencing a sense of efficacy with respect to providing assistance to a peer can be quite powerful. When the group itself includes people at various stages of their treatment process, those newer to the process may have a sense of hope they might not otherwise have when they hear from peers who have "been where they are" and know what it takes to overcome the struggles currently experienced by clients in earlier stages of treatment. Two final benefits overlap as part of the group therapy experience: interpersonal learning and self-understanding. Interpersonal learning involves each group member becoming more aware of how they impact and are impacted by other members of the group. Each group member receives feedback from both group members and group facilitator(s), which helps the group member understand the impact they have on others and how they may be affected by how other people behave. This type of learning is inextricably linked to self-understanding. When you get feedback and learn more about how you impact and are impacted by the world around you, you will learn more about and develop a greater understanding of yourself.

Generally, group therapy is most effective for those who are able to give and receive feedback and tolerate the stress that can come from interacting with others in this type of therapeutic setting. Because not everyone can benefit from or function effectively in group therapy, the group facilitator(s) will interview each potential group member prior to inclusion in the group. This will result in the facilitator(s)' decision to either include or exclude a group member. There are criteria that can be used to help facilitators determine who will be able to effectively function within the group therapy session, but that is beyond the scope of this book. Regardless, if a group therapy facilitator determines that a client is not a good fit for group therapy, they will explain why and make recommendations for other forms of therapy (i.e., individual, family, and couples) and provide referral sources the client can contact should they decide to do so.

Once the group is formed, the facilitator(s) will establish the ground rules of the group, which will include showing up on time, attending all sessions, and maintaining the privacy of each group member by not talking about other people's experience outside of the group therapy setting. The facilitator(s) will also explain whether the group is a closed group (no new members will be added) or an open group (new members will be added when there is room), how long each session will be, how many sessions the group will meet, and so on. Sometimes either at the start or throughout the group therapy process, the group itself may establish norms or rules that are expected of all group members. These expectations may be spoken or unspoken. Part of the task of the facilitator(s) would be to inquire about these expectations and determine if everyone is in agreement with them and how they will be implemented, including what will happen if someone breaks one of these rules or expectations. Regardless of the rules, who establishes them, and how they are established, it is important for all group members to understand what these expectations are so they can decide if they want to be part of such a group. When expectations evolve as the group meets, again these things would need to be explicitly identified and discussed to determine if the group agrees that the rule or expectation is a good one. For example, a group of patients with eating disorders may decide that they do not want to talk about specific "tricks" they use as part of their eating disorder or how much they weigh. These things may, in fact, be ground rules established by the facilitator; however, if they arise from group members, then a thorough discussion of the pros and cons of talking about or not talking about these issues should occur, with a decision made on how to move forward.

Finally, it is common for groups engaged in the group therapy process to go through predictable stages. There are five stages of group therapy, which include orientation (forming), power struggle (storming), cooperation and integration (norming), synergy (performing), and closure (adjourning). In the forming stage the group is getting to know one another and the expectations of the group, and look to the facilitator to keep the group on track and make decisions about what the group should discuss. In the storming stage group members may develop conflict and competition with one another. Oftentimes, the conflict and competition revolve around who the leader of the group is, how the group should be structured, who holds power in the group, and who is in a position of authority. It is not uncommon for group members to take on the role they normally take in their family of origin, which often accentuates conflict and dissention. This is a potentially fragile time for the group that must be handled with care so all group members feel valued and want to keep returning. During the third stage, norming, the group becomes more cohesive and readily acknowledges the contribution each member makes to the group. Group members start to show more flexibility in terms of how they view themselves and others as they hear other people's perspectives and recognize that various perspectives are neither better nor worse than another. The performing stage is not reached by all groups. During this fourth stage of group therapy, group members establish effective interdependence. Group members effectively interact with one another, provide feedback, offer solutions, and discuss difficult topics that arise among group members—all without much input from the facilitator(s). They are able to problem-solve and resolve group conflict among themselves with minimal input from facilitators. The final stage, adjourning, is characterized by working on ending the group. This is not as simple as counting down the number of sessions until the final one, although it is beneficial for this to occur as a reminder that the group will come to an end. With the end in mind, issues related to loss can arise and may become the focus of some final sessions. Group members are encouraged to discuss what it feels like to end the group with the understanding that relationships have been established that may or may not continue beyond the ending of the group. Thus, a major task of the group during this stage is planning how to say goodbye when we often do not have or take the opportunity to do so in real life.

17. What is family therapy?

Family therapy is usually understood in terms of how many members of a family are present during a therapy session; however, what truly distinguishes family therapy from individual therapy is the perspective a family therapist takes.

Family therapists or marriage and family therapists (MFTs) do not view any one individual as the client even if the family has identified a particular member of the family as the one "causing problems." Rather, an MFT views any problems as residing in the system or the family interactions as a whole—thus the entire system or family is the client. It is not always possible or necessary for all family members to be present during therapy sessions; however, since the intention is to heal the system, having as many members of that system as possible involved in the therapy process is best. While most people consider the family to be those living under the same roof, this is not always the case. Sometimes members of the family in the context of family therapy may or may not be related (i.e., by blood, adoption, fostering, or marriage) and may or may not live in the same household. Rather, a family member is considered to be anyone who plays an important role in someone's life providing support in one way or another.

Common reasons that families might seek family therapy include situations in which one person in the family is dealing with a significant mental or medical illness that disrupts healthy family functioning. The treatment is not focused on the individual with the illness but on how the family system itself has been affected by the illness or may maintain the illness. Other reasons for those seeking family therapy will include any events that disrupt effective family interactions such as divorce, domestic violence, conflict between parents, moving, natural disaster, and loss of a family member.

When family therapy is either recommended or something that a patient is looking for, it is important to find a clinician who has specific training in this form of therapy. The clinician will more than likely be a licensed marriage and family therapist (see Question 4); however, the license alone does not indicate what type of family therapy a particular clinician may practice. There are several different approaches to marriage and family therapy; some of the most common are briefly described in the following paragraphs.

Family therapists who practice using Murray Bowen's approach, Bowenian therapy, will focus on concepts such as triangulation and differentiation. Triangulation refers to the idea that when someone is experiencing conflict with another member of the family, they will pull in a third member of the family (which completes the triangle) to help them feel better about themselves. This is common, for example, among parents who may be struggling with one another. Instead of trying to solve the problem directly with their (ex)spouse, they may triangulate a third member of the family, often a child, by complaining to the child about the other parent or by trying to get the child to side with them. Differentiation has to do with the degree to which individuals can emotionally separate themselves from their family members. Undifferentiated members of the family will get pulled into emotional drama or conflict much more easily than differentiated family members. For example, an undifferentiated adult child will not be able to tolerate conflict or criticism from another family member without reacting strongly emotionally by lashing out, engaging in an argument, and so on. Thus, Bowenian family therapy seeks to address these and other dynamics in the family system to develop or restore healthy interactions.

Structural family therapy, developed by Salvador Minuchin, focuses on the structure or hierarchy within the family. When the power structure in the family is out of balance, there can be conflict and unhealthy interactions. Structural family therapists will evaluate the family in terms of what role each family member has in the family and which family members hold power. The therapist will then work with the family to restore power where it belongs and address problematic roles. For example, in a family where the child "runs" the family (e.g., decisions are made based on what the child wants rather than what the parents believe is best), a structural family therapist will work with the parents, and the child(ren), to reestablish appropriate decision-making power with the parents. Another concern when there are two parents or guardians is to ensure that those two family members work together to set reasonable limits with children.

The family therapy approach developed by Gianfranco Cecchin-Milan is referred to as systemic family therapy. This approach utilizes one of the major concepts from the psychoanalytic and psychodynamic approaches (see Questions 7 and 8, respectively): the unconscious mind. Systemic family therapy assumes that what a family may be communicating with one another may take place at an unconscious level. That is, the meaning behind the communication among family members may not be obvious and therefore the systemic family therapist will help the family determine what their communication means. Power in the family, for example, is interpreted to reflect the unconscious "game" family members are engaged in. Power within the family is therefore seen as something that perpetuates the family problem rather than being the problem in and of itself. Ultimately, the goal is to help the family find more productive ways of interacting, which promotes growth within the family system.

Strategic family therapy, developed by Jay Haley, takes a brief approach to working with families, meaning work in this form of therapy is direct and takes place over a relatively short period of time (e.g., weeks or two to three months rather than six months to a year or more). Direct, brief approaches, such as this one, often utilize homework assignments designed to help improve family interactions. Issues often involve hierarchy and power, which members of the family are aligned (i.e., who is teamed up), and how effectively family members communicate. In this approach it is not uncommon for the family therapist to identify the problem (e.g., a lot of arguing) and tell the family, as part of their homework, to argue more. This helps the family to understand that the problem is more within their control than they might think. If they can engage in the problem on purpose, then they are likely able to stop it as well.

Many MFTs, regardless of the approach they take, may use a *genogram* as a way to assess the nature of the family structure and interactions. In its most basic form the genogram is like a family tree that contains more information. A family tree shows who is related to whom and how (e.g., who are the grandparents, who is part of the family by marriage). The genogram also includes information such as whether relationships between specific family members are strained, who is living together, who is separated or divorced, who is in a sexual relationship, and whether there is abuse. The genogram will also include information about disorders (e.g., substance abuse, anxiety) or diseases (e.g., diabetes, cardiovascular disease). Essentially, the genogram can include any information that is deemed important by the therapist and/or the family members and that affects how family members interact. Genograms can be used in couples counseling, individual counseling, or family therapy. When used in family therapy, it can be useful to compare genograms created by members of the same family. Discrepancies may point to important issues that affect how family members understand and relate to one another.

For example, if one child and one parent identifies the other parent as an alcoholic but that parent and another child does not, this indicates that the perception of that family member and his or her struggles is not perceived the same way and may also illustrate which family members are aligned with one another.

18. What is evidence-based practice?

"Evidence-based practice" is a term that is derived from the field of medicine (evidence-based medicine) and that has since been adopted by other disciplines in the broader field of health care such as counseling and therapy. Evidence-based practice is differentiated from evidence-based therapy which focuses on identifying which therapies are effective at treating specific disorders or concerns (see also Question 19). In 2006 the American Psychological Association (APA; the largest professional organization of psychologists in the United States) published a paper entitled "Evidence-Based Practice in Psychology." It provided a brief history of the concept of evidence-based practice along with a definition and thorough discussion of each part of the definition.

Evidence-based practice is defined by the APA as "the integration of the best available research with clinical expertise in the context of patient characteristics, culture, and preferences." It noted that this definition is similar to the one adopted by medical professionals but that the APA's statement deepens the understanding and impact of both clinical expertise and client factors. There are three primary components to this definition, and the analogy used to describe evidence-based practice is a three-legged stool: if you remove one leg, the stool will not remain upright. The implication is that removing any one of the three elements from a professional's practice will mean that they are not providing their client with the best treatment possible.

The component "best available research evidence" refers to the idea that any treatment intervention must have a solid research foundation showing that the intervention is effective. This means that numerous scientific studies have been conducted using a variety of research designs (e.g., randomized control trials, case studies, clinical observations, meta-analysis) that, in aggregate, show the intervention of study is effective at treating a wide variety of diagnoses (or a specific diagnosis) in child, adolescents, and/or adults.

"Clinical expertise" is another leg in the three-legged stool and refers to a variety of competencies that practicing psychologists and many of those in other professions (e.g., counseling, marriage and family therapy) receive education and training in. There are myriad elements to clinical expertise that include a clinician's ability to effectively use assessment, diagnosis, case formulation, and treatment planning when working with a patient. Other factors include clinical decision-making, monitoring patient progress, interpersonal expertise, evaluation and use of research findings, self-reflection, understanding the influences of differences between individuals and among different cultures, seeking assistance (e.g., supervision, consultation) when needed, and being able to articulate why the therapist used a particular intervention or treatment strategy. Essentially, clinical expertise refers to the idea that the counselor or therapist is well trained to identify and formulate a treatment plan for a particular patient and their needs, and knows why they are using that particular treatment strategy with that particular patient.

Finally, the element of "patient characteristics, culture, and preferences" points to the importance of knowing who the client is and what may or may not be a good fit for them. That is, the best research evidence and exceptional clinical expertise leading a therapist to decide on a particular course of treatment do not mean that form of treatment will work for that particular patient. Individual differences in this context can refer to gender, gender identity, culture, ethnicity, age, religious beliefs, sexual orientation, and so on. These and other factors that make each of us unique affect how we develop and how we function as we age. Moreover, regardless of what among those factors may affect a particular patient, the patient may have strong preferences for what type of therapy they do or do not want to be part of. It is not uncommon for some patients, for example, to want a solution to a specific issue. In that case they would likely prefer a solution-focused form of treatment (e.g., behavioral therapy, cognitive behavioral therapy; see Questions 9 and 11, respectively) rather than an insight-oriented form of treatment (e.g., psychodynamic psychotherapy; see Question 8). By contrast, those who want to understand why they have the concerns they have may prefer an insight-oriented form of treatment.

19. Is one type of therapy better than another?

When considering the question of whether one form of therapy is better or more effective than another, there are a multitude of factors to consider. Three primary factors often used to decide which therapy to use with a particular client are (1) the best-available research; (2) clinical expertise; and (3) patient characteristics, culture, and preferences (see Question 18). Another set of factors used to determine which form of therapy is effective has less to do with the specific type of treatment (see Questions 7–18) and more to do with factors that may be involved in all forms of treatment. These factors may help explain why there are so many forms of therapy (there are dozens more than what has been described in this book) and why more than one therapy has been shown to be effective in treating the same disorders. These factors are called *common factors* and include, but are not limited to, the alliance, empathy, expectations, cultural adaptation of evidence-based treatments, and therapist effects.

The alliance is among the more robust factors that seems to affect the outcome of therapy. This means that this factor is strongly connected to whether therapy will be effective. The alliance refers to the relationship or bond that exists between the therapist and the patient, the agreement about goals for therapy, and the agreement about what should be done to reach those goals (i.e., what tasks need to be completed). When the patient and therapist have a strong collaborative relationship, and they agree on the goals and tasks of therapy, there is a strong chance that the outcome of therapy will be beneficial for the patient. That is, he or she will have achieved the goals they had hoped to achieve as a result of seeing a therapist.

Empathy, which is a factor of paramount importance in client-centered therapy (see Question 14), has been found to be quite important to the process of effective therapy. Empathy refers to the capacity of one person (in this case the therapist) to share the emotional state of another person (the patient) and to be able to take on the other person's perspective. When a therapist is able to have empathy for a patient, they are able to fully and deeply understand what the patient is feeling and why they are feeling that way. Oftentimes, the therapist is able to demonstrate their understanding of the patient by describing what the patient must be experiencing using words and descriptors the patient hadn't used. For example, a client may say they are afraid and the therapist may say that the patient appears to be terrified. Research has routinely found that empathy and the other important concepts from client-centered therapy (i.e., acceptance and genuineness) are strongly connected to a positive outcome of therapy.

Expectations in the context of therapy have to do with the degree to which the client expects the therapy to work. Some patients may enter therapy with the expectation that it will work because they've experienced effective therapy previously or they simply trust that it will be effective. The expectation that therapy will work is often created from the therapist's explanation of what is going with a patient and why, providing an explanation of what form of therapy will be used and why, and the direct participation in the therapy itself. Expectations of the effectiveness of therapy have been shown to affect the outcome of treatment such that when a patient expects therapy will work there is a greater chance that the therapy will, in fact, work. These findings are not as strong as those for the alliance and empathy but do seem to be an important factor in understanding why therapy works.

Finally, the factor "therapist effects" points to the notion that who the therapist is and how they deliver treatment affects the outcome of therapy. In short, this factor suggests that some therapists are better than others. Although the finding that some therapists may be better than others has been established for some time, what has been less clear is what it is about these effective therapists that differentiates them from less effective therapists. Recently some researchers have attempted to parse out what those characteristics might be. Effective therapists have been found to do a better job forming a strong alliance regardless of who the patient is and what their concerns are, have more well-developed interpersonal skills (i.e., the ability to understand and send interpersonal messages and to effectively explain what the problem is and why it developed, along with what solutions are likely to work), are more likely to express professional self-doubt (i.e., question whether what they are doing is the right thing or the most helpful thing), and spend more time outside of the therapy setting practicing therapeutic skills (e.g., active listening, empathy).

Although there is research indicating that in some cases specific forms of treatment are truly better than others for a specific diagnosis (e.g., *systematic desensitization* for the treatment of phobias), there is a great deal of research suggesting that what is more important than the type of therapy used is whether the therapist and patient can form a strong alliance, whether the therapist can display empathy along with acceptance and genuineness, and the degree to which both the therapist and, more important, the patient believe the therapy will work.

Deciding to Seek Counseling and Finding a Counselor

20. Should I seek individual, couples, family, or group therapy?

Determining whether to seek individual, couples, family, or group therapy is determined, in part, by what the problem or concern is and potentially who is affected by it. You may have some idea on your own regarding which mode of therapy is appropriate; however, it is also possible that after meeting with an individual, couples, family, or group therapist, that therapist may make a recommendation for another mode of therapy that can more effectively assist you and/or your loved ones (e.g., spouse, child, roommate, other family members).

Individual therapy is one-on-one therapy, meaning only you and the therapist meet for your sessions. This mode is appropriate for those who have issues or concerns they want to work on without the involvement of another loved one. Your issues may impact others; however, you and/ or your therapist have determined that working on some or all of the issues in a one-on-one setting will be the most effective mode of therapy. It is possible that a therapist may recommend another mode of therapy in addition to or instead of individual therapy despite the fact that you may not wish to involve anyone else. Your individual therapist will likely talk with you about your thoughts and feelings about involv-ing others in therapy as well as let you know why they think another mode (e.g., couple counseling) would be beneficial. Ultimately, it is up to you. Your current therapist may say that they cannot help you in the way that you need and may refer you to another individual therapist, but it is still up to you whether you want to pursue another mode of therapy.

Couples counseling is often referred to as marriage counseling since a married couple is the most likely to be taking part in this mode of therapy. Couples counseling involves two people seeking counseling and one or two therapists. The two people seeking counseling are usually involved in an intimate relationship. This does not necessarily refer to a physically or sexually intimate relationship but can also mean an emo-tionally intimate relationship. The idea is that you and another person share a great deal with one another and the relationship is very import-ant to you both. Any problems in the relationship, therefore, would be appropriate for couples counseling. Therefore, in addition to married couples, the clients in couples counseling may be two people who are dating, who are roommates, who are best friends, and so on. Couples counseling often addresses communication issues in the relationship revolving around establishing clear communication and learning how to effectively listen to what the other person is communicating. A cou-ple may be assisted in this mode of therapy by one or two therapists. The most likely scenario is that there is one therapist who is the therapist for the couple (i.e., the couple is the client/patient not either person individually). This therapist will certainly address issues one person may have in session but only to the extent that those issues are part of the couple's issue. For example, someone who has a trauma history may need assistance in couples counseling with their spouse on how to ask for what they need so that they are not inadvertently re-traumatized. If, how-ever, the effects of the individual's trauma are so powerful that they need to be dealt with prior to the couple's work being effective, the couples therapist will likely recommend that the person see a different therapist for individual counseling at the same time couples counseling is occur-ring, or it may be recommended that they seek individual therapy first before couples counseling. When there are two therapists involved in couples counseling, it is often the case that the co-counselors will match the gender of the two clients. Therefore, if the couple is both females, then the two counselors would be female. If one is female and one is male, then there would be one male and one female counselor. Though matching the sex of the clients this way is not required, it can be helpful for the clients to feel someone in the room may share their perspective (especially in the case of a male–female couple). In addition, a benefit of having co-counselors for this mode of therapy is that they can model effective communication and problem solving. Both counselors are not always going to agree on a particular direction to take in therapy. Thus, they can discuss this openly in session and come to some kind of a compromise or mutually agreed-upon resolution. This demonstrates to the couple that disagreement can occur and can be resolved peacefully and amicably.

Family therapy involves multiple members of a family and one therapist. Although most people likely think of the parent(s) and child(ren) when considering who the family is, the reality is that a family in this context is typically defined based on who shares a home. Therefore, the family may consist of parents and their children, grandparents, aunts or uncles, and so on. It may also include nonfamily members who live in the family's household full-time (e.g., a friend of one of the children who lives with the family permanently). Family can also be defined in terms of a divorced couple with children who are remarried with or without other children. Depending on what the issue or concern is, the family in family therapy in this instance may include the divorced couple, their shared children, their new spouses (stepparents to the children), and any additional children who may be affected by the current concern. Similar to couples counseling in which the couple is the client, in family therapy the family is the client. The idea is to help the family function more effectively for everyone involved. There may be an identified patient (IP), which means one particular member of the family is struggling in such a way that their behaviors are disruptive to the family and are distressing to the family members. If that is the case, then the IP would likely have individual counseling where the focus is on his or her concerns and the family therapy would be focused on how the family as a whole can cope with and manage the IP's behaviors and any other concerns that arise.

Group therapy is similar to family therapy, in that there are more than two people meeting for therapy, and there may be one or two therapists involved. In group therapy the group is not necessarily the client as with couples or family therapy since the group itself typically does not exist outside of the group therapy context. In fact, a requirement of participating in some forms of group therapy is that group members cannot socialize outside of group therapy as that can detract from the work that happens in group therapy itself. The group is usually brought together based on a shared concern. For example there may be group therapy for depression, eating disorders, low self-esteem, bereavement, and so on. Theoretically group therapy can have any theme for which there would be enough people interested in participating. The ideal size for group therapy is 8–10 clients. Clients are usually individuals, but it is possible to have group therapy for couples. In that case the couple is the client, and there may be 8–10 couples participating in the group. The benefits of group therapy are many and include the fact that the individual or couple is in a room with people who have similar concerns. This can help people feel less alone and isolated as it is common for individual clients to believe they are the only one dealing with the issues and concerns they have. Another benefit of group therapy is that there is an opportunity for individuals or couples to help one another. Part of the group therapy experience is the interactions that take place between group members. This is often commented on and processed by the therapist or co-therapists; however, it is possible that after the group has met for some time a group member can help facilitate an interaction between other group members. The group member can also help with solutions to problems that they have previously encountered. The presence of one or two therapists is similar to couples therapy, in that either is sufficient; however, given the preference of the therapist(s) or the nature of the group, it may make sense for only one or two therapists to be involved. If there are two therapists, they may both be present at each session, may alternate sessions, or come up with some other preplanned arrangement for who will attend which groups. The group would be made aware of this in advance. It is also beneficial to have two therapists in the event that one therapist cannot attend due to illness or some other obligation; the group session would not have to be canceled and would be facilitated by the other therapist on their own.

21. What is the difference between outpatient therapy and inpatient therapy?

In the simplest terms, the difference between outpatient therapy (OP) and inpatient therapy (IP) has to do with where the therapy takes place. OP takes place in a therapist's or counselor's office, whereas IP takes place in a hospital after you are admitted as a patient. There are some other variations that will be discussed.

Receiving OP usually means your symptoms are not so severe that you cannot adequately function in your daily life with minimal support.

Typically weekly sessions are all that are needed. Sometimes if someone's symptoms increase in severity or they experience a crisis in a particular week, they may meet with their outpatient therapist two times in one week. Typically meetings with an outpatient therapist do not exceed twice per week—this is usually due to the limitations of health insurance (see Questions 40–44 for more information about insurance), which often states that they will not cover OP counseling or therapy sessions beyond two sessions per week. Exceptions may be made if there is an acute crisis and the patient feels they need to be seen sooner than their next regularly scheduled appointment.

Inpatient therapy is reserved for those cases in which someone's symptoms are so severe that they require care 24 hours a day. In these instances the individual is admitted to a hospital as a patient (just as someone would be admitted to the hospital for a medical issue). The length of time someone will remain an inpatient is determined, in part, by how severe the patient's symptoms are, by the degree to which they may be a danger to themselves (i.e., suicidal) or someone else (i.e., homicidal, or intending to do serious harm to someone else), and by their insurance coverage (see Questions 40–44 for more information about insurance). Many insurance companies will have a limit to how long a patient can stay in a hospital based on the specific diagnosis. In other instances the limit may be based on the diagnosis in part but also the degree to which the patient's symptoms are improving. For example, someone with a diagnosis of anorexia nervosa may be admitted to a hospital as an inpatient because their medical health is deteriorating. How long that patient stays in the hospital depends on improvement of their vital signs, which would include weight gain in this instance. Once the patient is determined to be medically stable and not a threat to themselves or anyone else, the insurance company may state that they will no longer cover inpatient services and the patient would need to be discharged (or pay for the extra hospital stay out of pocket—see Question 42 for an explanation of this and insurance-related terms).

There are variations for both OP and IP. A form of OP that provides additional assistance to a patient who does not meet the requirements for a hospital admission but needs more support than weekly or biweekly sessions is called intensive outpatient therapy (IOP). IOP usually involves taking part in therapy for several hours a day, several days a week. The therapy usually is in the form of group therapy that focuses on skill building for communication skills, self-esteem issues, and diagnosis-specific skills such as relapse prevention for those dealing with substance abuse.

Sometimes individual therapy is part of the intensive outpatient program; other times the outpatient therapist is someone not affiliated with the program and provides the therapy as an additional form of treatment and support for the individual.

Inpatient treatment that differs from that described earlier in this section is called partial hospitalization—sometimes referred to as partial for short. This form of treatment is affiliated with a hospital and is often a step down from inpatient hospitalization. It serves as a transition from 24/7 care to something that provides more oversight than intensive outpatient treatment would provide. With partial hospitalization the individual is not admitted as a patient to stay overnight, as with inpatient hospitalization. In this instance the individual is a patient of the hospital but is receiving treatment most hours of the day, every day of the week (usually excluding weekends), and stays overnight somewhere else (e.g., the individual's home, a hotel, temporary lodging provided by the hospital). This form of treatment provides more support than someone would receive if they were part of an intensive outpatient program, and they are also usually monitored medically. This means that they will regularly meet with a nurse and/or physician who will monitor their vital signs and order additional tests if needed to ensure their medical well-being.

Both intensive outpatient treatment and partial hospitalization are time-limited by design (e.g., the program may be designed to last for three weeks) or based solely on how well the patient is coping in the context of the treatment they are currently receiving. If someone was inpatient for a mental health concern, it is common that once discharged from inpatient treatment they will be transitioned to partial hospital or intensive outpatient and then to outpatient only.

One final form of treatment that is usually set up for specific disorders such as substance use disorders or eating disorders is the residential treatment facility. These facilities are residential in nature, which means the individual would live at the treatment facility until their treatment was completed. This type of treatment is used for those whose symptoms are severe enough that outpatient treatment of any kind is not sufficient, but they are not medically compromised and therefore do not need to be admitted for inpatient treatment. When someone receives residential treatment, it usually means they receive individual therapy, group therapy, family therapy, medical monitoring, medication monitoring, and other services such as art therapy, occupational therapy, and equine (horse) therapy. These treatment facilities tend to be very expensive and are paid for by insurance companies only if a case can be made for their medical necessity (see Question 42 for a description of this and other insurance-related terms).

22. What is a mental health diagnosis, and what does it mean?

A mental health diagnosis can also be referred to as a psychiatric diagnosis, a mental illness, a mental disorder, a psychiatric disorder, or a psychiatric illness. Whatever term is used, it means that the individual is experiencing symptoms severe enough that they are causing impairment in some way in their everyday life and require treatment for their symptoms.

Mental health diagnoses in the United States are determined using the *Diagnostic and Statistical Manual of Mental Disorders* (DSM), which is published by the American Psychiatric Association. The most recent version is the *DSM-5*, which was published in 2013. Worldwide, most other health-care providers use the *International Classification of Diseases* (ICD), which includes both mental health and medical diagnoses. The most recent version is the *ICD-10*, with the updated *ICD-11* anticipated to be in use by 2022.

Mental health diagnoses are grouped into categories or classifications. According to the *DSM* there are 20 categories of diagnoses, which are neurodevelopmental disorders, schizophrenia spectrum and other psychotic disorders, bipolar and related disorders, depressive disorders, anxiety disorders, obsessive-compulsive and related disorders, trauma- and stressor-related disorders, dissociative disorders, somatic symptom disorders, feeding and eating disorders, elimination disorders, sleep–wake cycle disorders, sexual dysfunctions, gender dysphoria, disruptive impulse control and conduct disorders, substance use and addictive disorders, neurocognitive disorders, personality disorders, paraphilic disorders, and other disorders.

The use of a specific mental health diagnosis helps both patients and health-care providers talk about and describe what the patient is experiencing. The proper identification of a disorder will also mean that an appropriate and effective form of treatment can be implemented. For some people, knowing what their diagnosis is gives them peace of mind that there is an explanation for what they are going through and that they can be helped. Others, however, may be concerned about the stigma associated with mental illness and feel they are a failure or are weak for having such a problem. They may even worry about what their treatment provider thinks of them based on their diagnosis (see Question 6 for additional information about this type of concern).

Others have criticized the use of mental health diagnosis because the nature of diagnosis simplifies and objectifies who the person is and what they are going through. Over the years mental health diagnoses have changed—some have been added, some have been removed. The changes, especially when a new disorder is added, leave some to wonder where society draws the line between normal behavior that does not require treatment but may be disruptive (e.g., a highly active child who does not have ADHD in a school setting) and a mental illness that requires treatment for the quality of life of the individual.

Regardless of one's view of the usefulness of mental health diagnoses, only someone trained in mental health diagnosis and treatment has sufficient knowledge to determine when a particular diagnosis is appropriate and to differentiate between diagnoses that may have some symptoms in common (see Questions 3 and 4 for more information about types of counselors and their credentials).

23. Do I need to see a counselor who has a particular specialty?

When a health-care provider has a specialty of some kind, it means that they have had specific education, training, and supervision to work effectively with a particular diagnosis or concern. Generally, you are not required to work with someone who is a specialist in the area of your concerns; however, if available, a specialist is likely to better understand the complexities of your concerns and to identify the most effective approaches to treatment compared to a nonspecialist.

Determining whether a counselor or psychotherapist has a specialty can be as simple as checking out their website for any listed specialties or by asking them via a phone call when you are initially determining if they are a good fit for you and your concerns (see Questions 1–6 and 26 for more information on finding a counselor or therapist). A therapist who states that they have a particular specialty, however, does not necessarily mean they have had sufficient education, training, and supervision to ethically allow themselves to declare a particular specialty. It is, therefore, important to search for information on or ask directly about what credentials they have for their specialty. It is within the realm of possibility that there is not a credential for a particular specialty; however, the counselor or psychotherapist should be able to elaborate on what education, training, and supervision they did receive and from where to justify their particular expertise.

Some specialty areas do have credentials or a set of guidelines that outline what education and experiences a specialist in a particular area should have to ethically call themselves a specialist. For example, the American Psychological Association has documents that outline criteria for specific specialty areas. These documents include, but are not limited to, *Specialty Guidelines for Forensic Psychology*, *Guidelines for Child Custody Evaluations in Family Law Proceedings*, *Guidelines for the Psychological Practice with Older Adults*, and *Guidelines for Assessment of and Intervention with Persons with Disabilities*. Other organizations offer certifications based on certain criteria they deem necessary for ethical practice in a particular area. For example, the International Association for Eating Disorder Professionals certifies licensed mental health professionals as certified eating disorder specialists if they meet an extensive list of criteria. In addition, some insurance companies have a list of particular specialties for which they require licensed mental health professionals to prove they have the right credentials or have extensive education, training, and supervision in a particular area. These may include disorders such as autism spectrum disorders, eating disorders, substance use disorders, and pain management. Insurances may also include particular demographics or particular forms of treatment among their list of specialties. This may include, but is not limited to, neuropsychological testing, working with specific age groups, using dialectical behavioral therapy (DBT), or eye movement desensitization and reprocessing (EMDR).

If you are not sure if it possible to formally specialize in the area of your particular concern, you can conduct an Internet search including the name of or brief description of your concern along with the word "specialty" (e.g., PTSD specialty). In addition, each state has a professional board that licenses mental health professionals. You can contact the board for a particular license in your state and ask if professionals with that license can have a specialty in treating your diagnosis or area of concern. You can find the right board by doing an Internet search for your state and the profession you're interested in. For example, search using phrases such as "state of Maine" and "psychology board" or "state of New York" and "counseling board" to find contact information.

24. What should I ask a counselor before I decide to schedule an appointment?

There are a number of things you can ask a counselor or psychotherapist before scheduling an appointment. Many of these things are practical in nature, while others address questions such as whether a counselor will be a good fit for you and your concerns (see Question 5 for more information on finding the right counselor).

One of the first questions you can ask a potential counselor is whether they are accepting new patients/clients at this time. Although the counselor will tell you as soon as possible if they are not, if this is the first thing you ask you can determine quickly whether it makes sense to explain your concerns and why you are seeking counseling. If you are using insurance, the second thing you can ask is whether the counselor accepts your health-care insurance (see Questions 40–44 for more information on using insurance). Even if they say they do not, it still may be possible for you to afford to work with them if you determine otherwise that they are a good fit. If they do not accept your insurance, you can ask if they have a sliding scale fee structure. This means that they have a usual and customary amount they charge (see Question 41 for an explanation of this term) but lower their fee under certain circumstances (e.g., based on income, based on number of sessions you may need). In addition, even if they do not take your insurance and your insurance plan covers mental health services, you can submit claims to the insurance company for reimbursement (see Questions 40 and 41 for more information about these insurance-related issues). Your counselor should provide you with all the information you need to accurately complete whatever form your insurance company requires so you can get reimbursed for part of the cost of your sessions.

Assuming the counselor is taking on new patients and you have determined that they take your insurance or you can otherwise afford to see this counselor, it is then important to inquire about their ability to work with your particular concern. You may know what your diagnosis is (or have an idea of what it is) and you can share that information, or you can provide a brief description of what you are experiencing and how it affects you. For example, you might say something like "I feel anxious a lot of the time and have a really hard time keeping my thoughts together. I feel like my thoughts won't slow down or be quiet. Is that the kind of thing you can help me with?" If the counselor does not work with the type of diagnosis or concern you described, then you can ask if there is someone else to whom they can refer you. Usually the counselor will have some idea of who in the area is likely to work with the types of concerns you have.

If the counselor says that they do work with the concerns you've described, you can then ask about their approach to counseling when working with these types of issues. If you are knowledgeable about different counseling approaches, you can ask them what type of treatment they do or what approach they use (see Questions 7–19 for information about different therapy approaches). If you are unfamiliar with the different approaches to therapy, you can ask how they usually work with someone with the concerns you have. For example, you could ask questions like "What do you do?" "How do you go about helping someone like me?" or "How many sessions do you think I'll need?" Based on the counselor's answer to these types of questions, you will start to get a feel for what it might be like to work with this person. Of course, you won't really know that until you meet with the counselor directly; however, if the counselor provides a description of their approach to your concerns that just doesn't sound right to you, or makes you feel uncomfortable, you can certainly ask follow-up questions such as "I've never heard of that before, can you tell me more about it?" or "That sounds like it might make me feel worse, does that happen with other people you work with?" Essentially, you can ask any follow-up question you need to if you feel confused or you need more information to make a decision. If the counselor has appropriately and respectfully answered your questions and you're still not sure you can do one of two things, (1) go ahead and schedule an initial appointment to see how things feel face-to-face or (2) thank them for their time and call other counselors and ask them the same questions. If you find that you are unsure about all of the counselors you call, it is possible that you may be nervous or wary about counseling, in general, and may need to schedule an appointment with someone so you can experience what counseling feels like.

Ultimately, whether you work with any counselor is up to you. You may think after a phone conversation that the counselor is a good fit for you but do not get that impression when meeting face-to-face. It is acceptable to discontinue meeting with a counselor for that reason since your degree of comfort in counseling can help determine whether counseling will be effective for you. It's always a good idea to talk about any discomfort you are feeling as the counselor may be able to adjust their approach to better fit your needs or make a referral to someone who might be a better fit.

25. Why is my counselor asking me to provide information (on the initial paperwork) about things that have nothing to do with why I'm going to counseling?

Most counselors and therapists will have you complete paperwork before your first session often referred to as intake paperwork. This is requested not only to get contact information and insurance information but to also get a sense of your current concerns and any history of treatment you may have. All of this likely makes a lot of sense for your counselor to have, particularly providing them with information about why you are coming to therapy and if you've ever received treatment before. The information can help inform your counselor about whether treatment has worked for you before and whether you found it to be valuable. However, this initial paperwork often includes questions about things that may seem completely unrelated to why you set up your appointment to begin with.

It is common to be asked about any other psychiatric diagnoses you may have now or have previously been diagnosed with. Similarly, you may be asked if anyone else in your family has ever been diagnosed with a psychiatric disorder and, if so, what the disorder was. Knowing your and your family's history of mental illness can help your counselor determine whether a particular diagnosis makes sense for you—many diagnoses can be genetically inherited—or if another disorder should be considered. Since some disorders overlap in terms of what symptoms are included, it can be helpful to know what those in your genetic family tree have been diagnosed with. This can help your counselor rule out or rule in particular diagnoses. For example, you may have symptoms that suggest the diagnosis of major depressive disorder (i.e., depression), but you have a family history of bipolar disorder. Knowing this history may prompt your counselor to ask additional questions about symptoms related to bipolar disorder that you may not have thought to discuss since it didn't seem directly relevant. In addition, knowing what you may have already been diagnosed with in the past may confirm your counselor's ideas about what may be going on now and provide additional information about how you may be experiencing your current concerns. For example, if you set up an appointment for feelings related to anxiety about performing in front of others (e.g., giving speeches, competing in athletics, performing as a musician) and you have previously been diagnosed with agoraphobia, that may help explain your desire to avoid performing altogether and to stay in your home or apartment.

In addition to knowing your history with mental illness, your counselor may inquire about your medical history—both past medical issues and current medical issues. Since the mind and body are known to be inextricably linked, it is typically the case that when the mind suffers, so does the body and vice versa. Moreover, some medical illnesses and conditions can mimic or mask mental illness, so having a full medical history can help your counselor more accurately determine what is going on with you psychiatrically. Without having this history, it is possible for you to be misdiagnosed, which can affect treatment.

You may also be asked about prescription and nonprescription medications, other substances you use, or supplements you take. This can include how much caffeine you consume, how much you smoke, and what, if any, illicit drugs you use (e.g., cocaine). Since prescription and nonprescription drugs, substances, and herbal supplements can affect your brain and body chemistry, they can also affect your psychiatric functioning. Someone who is seeing a counselor for anxiety, for example, will likely hear that it is recommended they cut back or eliminate altogether any sources of caffeine (or other stimulants) since caffeine consumption is known to exacerbate symptoms of anxiety. In addition, many mental health diagnoses require ruling out whether the symptoms can be explained by the use of a substance. The idea is if the symptoms are connected to the substance, then when the substance is discontinued or reduced the symptoms will go away or will improve and therefore psychotherapy for the apparent diagnosis may not be necessary. Regardless, if someone is using substances that affect their overall functioning, counseling to address substance use or abuse is often beneficial.

Finally, knowing about any past treatment you have received whether for the same symptoms that brought you to your current counselor or for something else entirely can help inform your counselor regarding what may work best for you now. The amount and types of treatment may also let your counselor know how severe and/or chronic your concerns may be as well as what types of settings or approaches seemed to benefit you the most. This can allow your counselor to tailor counseling services to best meet your needs. Alternatively, this information may mean that your counselor recommends another method of treatment that the counselor does not provide. For example, you may have benefited in the past from family therapy and not benefited as much from individual therapy. Depending on what your concerns are, it may make sense to refer you to a family therapist or couples counselor if the current counselor does not provide that type of therapy.

26. What is a release of information (ROI) form, and why would my counselor ask me to sign one?

A release of information (ROI) is a form most health-care providers have that gives them permission to share relevant information with or receive information from someone else. An ROI is not usually required, but under some circumstances, it may be strongly encouraged or explicitly required in order for your counselor to work with you. For example, if you are dealing with medical issues of any severity, it may be important for your counselor to be able to talk with your medical provider to hear from them what your medical status is as well as how severe the symptoms are. Since the mind and body are connected, it can be helpful for your counselor to know what is going on with your physical well-being to better understand your mental well-being. In addition, in some cases, such as with eating disorders, it is often necessary for the counselor and medical provider to be in regular contact to help determine if the current mode of treatment (e.g., outpatient) is sufficient and whether a higher level of care such as residential or inpatient treatment is recommended.

The ROI is a form that gives one person permission to receive or share information with another person. At least one of the people involved is a health-care provider (i.e., your counselor), and the other person may be another health-care provider, family member, friend, coach, and so on. As the client you can request an ROI because you want your counselor to be able to talk to your physician, your parent, your best friend, your roommate, your priest, or whoever is important to you and has some information to share with regard to your current concerns. Alternatively, you may want the counselor to be able to talk to the other person so the counselor can share with them what is going on and talk with them about how to most effectively interact with you in ways that are more likely to help rather than hinder. Your counselor may make the request that you sign an ROI so that they can talk to someone else who provides treatment to you or who is otherwise in your life. If they made that request of you, they should also explain why they want to be able to talk to that person and how doing so will ultimately benefit you. Regardless of who asks for the ROI, it is a contract which means the person who signs the ROI and gives the counselor permission to talk with someone outside of your treatment is you as the patient if you are old enough and have the mental capacity to legally sign such a document, or is your legal guardian.

The ROI can be very broad, meaning you give your counselor permission to share anything related to your treatment, including your diagnosis, the counselor's summary of your work, and the counselor's impression of you and how the work is going. Or it can be very narrow and state that only certain details can be shared, such as whether you are attending sessions, how many sessions you have attended, and your formal diagnosis. The determination on how broad or how narrow the ROI will be is discussed between the counselor and the client and/or legal guardian.

The ROI also includes a section specifying how long it is good for. An ROI can last no longer than 1 year (12 months), which means if you are working with your counselor for more than 1 year and you want them to still be able to talk to the person for whom you originally signed the ROI, then another one will have to be completed and signed. The duration of the ROI can be as brief as however long it takes for the information to be shared. This means that the ROI is good for sharing information only once, and if additional information needs to be shared, then another ROI would have to be completed. Again, the length of the ROI would be determined via discussion between the client and the counselor.

Finally, signing an ROI does not mean you (or your legal guardian) cannot change your mind. All ROIs have a space for you to sign at any time you want to revoke the ROI. This means that you originally gave permission for your counselor and another person to share information but you have changed your mind and no longer want them to talk. You are allowed to do that at any time. Your counselor may talk with you about your reasoning and why it may still be beneficial to have the ROI in place; however, you (or your legal guardian) have the legal right to revoke that permission. It may make sense, however, to draw up a new ROI so that less information is shared rather than no information at all. That will depend on what is comfortable for you and what may benefit you and your treatment.

27. What should I expect at the first session?

The first session of counseling or therapy is usually referred to as an intake session. This means that a lot of background information is gathered, which will include what you are currently struggling with. This initial session may or may not be conducted with the person who will be your ongoing counselor.

An intake appointment includes paperwork and an initial counseling session. The paperwork may or may not be filled out at the initial appointment. Many counselors and mental health agencies make their intake paperwork available to clients ahead of time so that they can complete it prior to the appointment and do not need to take up any of their appointment time filling out forms. The paperwork itself will usually include a form that asks why you are seeking counseling. There is often space on such forms for you to write out what your concerns are. Some forms may have a symptom checklist that includes "low mood," "feeling anxious," "suicidal thoughts," "difficulty concentrating," and so on. You would circle or put a check next to any symptoms that apply to you. You may also be asked how serious or severe the symptoms are from your perspective—which is usually reflected by the degree to which the symptoms are interfering with your daily life and/or things that matter to you (see Question 1 for more information on determining whether you need counseling). This form may also include questions about past treatment you've received, current medications you take, medical issues, substances you use (which often include caffeine and tobacco), and so on. Although some of the questions may seem unrelated to why you are seeking counseling, providing this information can help your counselor more fully understand what may or may not be affecting you and/or your mental health symptoms. For example, some medications can induce mental health symptoms or make them worse. This can be the case, too, for some medical issues and substances.

Additional forms you will be asked to complete include an informed consent form, an HIPAA (Health Insurance Portability and Accountability Act) form, and possibly a release of information form. The informed consent form is a document that explains the policies and procedures (e.g., how cancelations are handled, how billing and payment are handled) of the counselor's practice or the agency where the counselor works. This form will also include information about under what circumstances the counselor is allowed to and not allowed to talk to other people about your counseling work (see Question 32 for more information about confidentiality). The HIPAA form is usually a brief document explaining how the counselor and/or the agency where the counselor works adhere to HIPAA regulations (see Question 36 for more information about HIPAA). You will be asked to sign both the informed consent and HIPAA forms acknowledging that you have read and understood the forms. You may also be asked to complete and sign a release of information (ROI) form (see Question 26 for more information on the ROI form), giving the counselor permission to talk with another person (usually a family member or another health-care provider) about your work with the counselor.

In addition to the paperwork, you will be asked to complete the first session, which is often an information-gathering session with respect to what has brought you to counseling. As noted earlier in the answer to this question, this information gathering session may or may not be conducted by the counselor with whom you will ultimately work. At larger agencies intake counselors see all new clients and go through a standardized interview process with the client. The intake counselor will ask a predetermined set of questions designed to get as clear a picture as possible about what your concerns are and what your mental health diagnosis might be. After that session you would be assigned to a counselor for ongoing counseling appointments. The counselor you are assigned to may be the one with the earliest appointment time, or the counselor may be someone with particular expertise that fits with your current concerns (e.g., someone with an eating disorder would benefit most from someone with a lot of training and experience working with individuals suffering from an eating disorder). Alternatively, the person with whom you meet at your initial session may be the same person who will be your counselor for ongoing sessions. This can occur at mental health agencies and is usually what will happen with a counselor in private practice. If your first session is with the counselor you will see for ongoing sessions they may take a structured approach just as the intake counselor would or they may take a more flexible approach. That is, the counselor may start with an open-ended question such as "What has brought you to counseling" and ask follow-up questions based on your answer, or the counselor may start with a more specific question based on information you provided in the paperwork, such as "You noted in the paperwork that you have been feeling sad for a long time. Can you tell me more about that?" The counselor may ask questions that are very specific, such as "Have you had any changes in eating?" or "Have you ever had a panic attack?" Questions such as these are designed to help the counselor narrow down the mental health diagnosis.

An additional element of the initial session is the establishment of goals. This may be done very explicitly and include statements like "I will have reduced _____ (an identified symptom) so that I can resume my regular work schedule." Sometimes the goals may be initially identified as the client wanting to feel better or not wanting to feel sad all the time. Goals such as these usually require further discussion either at the initial appointment or during later sessions as it is important for both the counselor and the client to know what feeling better would look and feel like for the client. Regardless, having clear goals allows both the counselor and client to know whether counseling is working and, if not, what adjustments need to be made or if additional forms of treatment need to be considered (e.g., medication—see Question 34 for more information about medication) so that the client is getting the help they need and want.

Although the end of the initial session can vary, it is customary for the counselor to inquire about setting up another appointment. The counselor may offer recommendations for how often to meet (e.g., every week, every two weeks) based on the client's concerns and how much these concerns are interfering with their daily life. It is also possible that the counselor may inquire as to the client's comfort with working with the counselor—the counselor would ask this in order to allow the client an opportunity to express any concerns they may have about working with the counselor. Usually this question is asked in the context of the importance of having a good fit so the client can benefit as much as possible. The counselor should also note that they are able to make a referral if for any reason the client does not feel they will be able to get what they need from this counselor.

28. How long is each appointment?

The standard counseling appointment is 45–50 minutes, with some exceptions based on what service is being provided and whether the session in question is the first session or a subsequent session.

A typical counseling appointment is often referred to as an hour; however, this is a bit misleading as the time spent with the counselor is usually 45–50 minutes. The remaining 10–15 minutes is set aside for the counselor to reflect on the session and write the session note. Record keeping is a pivotal part of the responsibility of a counselor—there are ethics and laws regulating record keeping for mental health services—and therefore time is needed to be sure an accurate record and summary of the session is kept. It is common for the initial session or intake session (see Question 27 for more information on the first session) to last 45–50 minutes like a regular counseling appointment; however, it is possible that the counselor may recommend a 90-minute appointment for the initial session since a great deal of background information is collected in addition to information about the client's current concerns. The 90-minute appointment is similar to the therapy "hour," in that the client will spend approximately 75 minutes with the counselor and the remaining time is set aside for record keeping.

Although the focus of this book is on counseling and psychotherapy, it is possible that in order to provide the best care possible the counselor may recommend a psychological assessment (see Question 33 for more information on psychological testing). If this recommendation is made, then the client will more than likely meet with another mental health professional (i.e., a psychologist), who specializes in psychological assessment. Based on why the assessment referral has been made, a battery of tests will be selected for the client to take. Depending on what tests and how many are used, an assessment appointment may last one to three hours. If the testing is extensive, the appointments may be spread out over more than one day, and each meeting may still last one to three hours.

Another possibility in terms of length of appointment has to do with crisis appointments. These appointments are typically made when the client needs to be seen prior to the next scheduled appointment time. Depending on the needs of the client, crisis appointments may be shorter than a standard appointment time (e.g., 20–30 minutes) so the counselor can assess the nature of the crisis and determine what services, if any, the client needs immediately (e.g., hospitalization). Alternatively, the crisis session may last for an hour or longer if it is determined that meeting with the counselor during an extended period of time can resolve the crisis, and the client can then wait until the next scheduled appointment. On some occasions, the crisis becomes apparent during a regularly scheduled appointment, and the session time is extended in order to resolve the crisis or to fully assess the nature of the crisis and arrange for additional services (e.g., another appointment the following day, referral to a psychiatric hospital).

29. How long should it take until I feel better?

The question regarding how long it will take before a client feels better is a good one, a common one, and one that is not so easy to answer. Although it is reasonable for your counselor to make a prediction about how long they expect to work with you on your current concerns—the implication being at the end of that time you'll feel better—the reality is there are so many factors that contribute to the course and outcome of counseling that a truly accurate prediction is, at best, difficult to make.

One of the most important factors involved in how long it may take before someone feels better has to do with how complex their concerns are. Complexity may be reflected in more than one mental health diagnosis (see Question 22 for more information on mental health diagnoses). When there is more than one mental health diagnosis, it may be possible to treat symptoms related to the diagnoses at the same time, and in other cases, it may be necessary for one to be treated before another one can realistically be addressed. This will depend, in part, on what the diagnoses are and how the diagnoses are affecting the client. The more severe the diagnosis, the more likely it is that a longer time will be needed before a client starts to feel better.

Sometimes complexity can be the result of poor social support, which may be the issue unto itself or may be a contributing factor to a client's current concerns. Therefore, treatment is focused on not only the symptoms related to the client's diagnosis but also discussing how to go about making changes in their social interactions. This can mean ending relationships with family members, an intimate partner, or friends, which are not healthy for the client. Making substantial changes such as this can impact many other areas of one's life, making the treatment process more complex with the possibility of new issues surfacing of which the client was not previously aware.

One issue related to how long it may take until a client feels better is whether the client recognizes they are getting better. It can be difficult to tell if you're feeling better in part because improvements may be slow going. Alternatively, it may be difficult to recognize you're getting better because you may be so accustomed to focusing on what is wrong that even when improvements are made you may still be focused on what is not yet better or what may not be as improved as you would like it to be. Regardless of the reason, one of the things a counselor can, and in some cases should, do is spend time on the fact that improvements have been made and specifically what those improvements are. For example, it can be helpful for the client when the counselor is able to say something like "When you first came to work with me you did not know what activities were enjoyable for you. Now you know what you like to spend your time on and you are working toward making sure you take time for those activities."

Another issue that makes the question of how long it will take to feel better somewhat difficult to answer has to do with how much better we're talking about. It is highly likely that a client will feel better after one session. This does not mean that they are where they want to be in terms of their overall well-being, but after having met with a counselor once, they may feel a sense of hope that what they are concerned about can be addressed and that they have someone to help them along the way. It will likely, however, take more time for the client to feel as well as they would like overall. In addition, the initial sense of well-being after one or two sessions can diminish rather quickly when the realization sets in that nothing yet has really changed.

A counselor is a highly trained and skilled professional who has the capacity to help in ways that will make most clients feel better; however, there is only so much a counselor can do. Ultimately, a lot of what contributes to a client feeling better is the client's ability to use the skills they are learning in their daily lives as well as the capacity to reflect on what is working for them and what is not. This is not to say that if a client is not feeling better, it is their fault—that is further from the truth. Rather, counseling or psychotherapy that is beneficial for the client involves an effective interaction between the counselor and the client. There are strategies and techniques the counselor should do to make sure a client feels safe and comfortable talking about whatever they need to (see Question 35 for information about what to do if you don't like your counselor and Question 5 for information on how to find the right counselor), and there is the type of work that only the client can do, such as talk about what they need to talk about, do some work in between sessions (e.g., specific "homework" agreed on in session, or time spent reflecting on what the client may have learned about themselves and how that affects them on a daily basis), and be motivated to make changes.

30. Why won't my therapist answer personal questions I ask them?

Different therapists will have different degrees of comfort with personal questions. Regardless, there can be a variety of reasons why your therapist will not answer personal questions, which can range from feeling uncomfortable with the specific question(s) asked to a policy to not answer any personal questions no matter what the question is and no matter which client asks. Ideally, however, your therapist will share their reasoning with you.

It is not uncommon for counselors and therapists to receive training to not disclose personal information about themselves even when and perhaps especially when a client asks them. The rationale for this typically revolves around the notion that the more a counselor reveals about themselves, the more a client may be distracted by knowing that information, and the focus of the sessions can shift. For example, as a client learns more about a counselor, they can start to feel as if they know who the counselor is and may develop a sense of friendship with the counselor. This can occur on the part of the counselor too. The danger of this happening is that the focus of the interactions can begin to move away from the work of counseling and from the client's concerns to talking about matters that two friends might talk about but that have nothing, or very little, to do with why the client sought counseling to begin with. Part of the shift that can occur as well is that some (or a lot) of the session time is spent talking about the counselor and how they are doing (because that's how conversations with friends often go), which means quite plainly that the client is spending their time and money talking about the counselor rather than themselves. This is, at best, not helpful for the client.

Because personal information about the counselor can be distracting in ways just discussed, some counselors take the position that they do not answer any personal questions no matter what. This, however, should be explained to the client either up front at the initial session (see Question 27 for more information about the first session) or when a personal question is asked of them. Without the explanation the client can be left feeling hurt and assuming that the counselor's lack of sharing in this regard is personal—the counselor is choosing to not share personal information with this client, whereas they might share personal information with other clients. Sometimes the decision to not share personal information with any client is made in the context of safety. Although the vast majority of clients do not pose a threat to a counselor, there are some clients who, if armed with personal information about the counselor, can use this information to cause psychological harm to the counselor or, if they learn enough about the counselor and are prone to antisocial behavior (i.e., the client does not care about the rights of other people), may make threats against the counselor and/or the counselor's family. Again this is exceedingly rare; however, it is possible and, therefore, some counselors may err on the side of extreme privacy.

Some counselors may be selective about what personal questions they answer. Thus, they are willing to answer some questions but will not answer others. The type of questions one chooses to answer or not will, of course, vary based on who the counselor is as well as their rationale for answering or not answering personal questions. Typically, however, when a personal question is answered under these conditions, it is done so only if doing so will benefit the client in some way. Sometimes, for example, it can be beneficial for a client to hear about a counselor's personal struggles and how they have coped with them, or a counselor may answer some personal questions for the explicit purpose of establishing rapport or a therapeutic connection with the client. Regardless, the discretion to answer or not answer any personal questions resides with the counselor in the same way that a client can choose to reveal or not reveal personal information to their counselor. Of course, the difference is that by not revealing personal information to the counselor, the client risks not getting the help they need.

Of course, it can be quite frustrating for some clients that the counselor knows a lot about them but they know very little about their counselor. This is, however, the nature of this type of work and what makes the nature of the relationship between the client and the counselor so important. If the relationship shifts too far from a professional helping someone in need, then the interactions may feel more like talking with a friend than talking with someone trained to help, and ultimately it is the client who will be harmed by that.

31. Therapy doesn't seem to be working—what should I do?

When we seek help for something, we want whatever help we receive to make us feel better. Thus, if the help we're receiving does not leave us feeling better, it makes sense to question what should be done: stick it out, walk away, find someone or something else, and so on. An additional question worth asking in the context of whether counseling is helping is, how long has it been? We live during a time when most things we want are easily and nearly immediately accessible—including some forms of medical care. Thus, it can be frustrating when what we want or even need takes time. Counseling can be something that takes more time than a client might like before they feel better (see Question 29 for more information about how long it may take before a client feels better) or before things start to feel as if they're working.

Regardless of timing or any other factors that may affect how much better you are feeling in the context of counseling, it is always a good idea to express your concerns to your counselor. Tell them that counseling does not seem to be working for you. Your counselor will likely ask you several questions to help clarify for them (and possibly for you) how counseling does not seem to be working. Your counselor may ask about what you had expected or hoped for and how it is different from the work you are doing with the counselor. Your counselor is also likely to ask you how you feel now and how you would like to feel, or how you had hoped to feel at this point. It is not uncommon for clients to make statements such as "I feel sad now and I no longer want to feel that way" or "I don't really know but I know I want to feel better than I do now." The later of the two statements is likely to prompt more clarifying questions about how you feel now and what you imagine "better" might feel like or look like. For example, the client may not be able to articulate their specific feelings but may be aware of something like "I just don't feel motivated to do anything right now, and I at least want to feel motivated to go to work again."

A client's sense of dissatisfaction is an excellent time to revisit the goals set at the beginning of the work (see Question 27 for more information about the first session). It is possible that the goals set at the outset of counseling were not the "right" goals. That does not mean that you or the counselor got it wrong at the beginning, but what it can mean is that as you have attended your counseling sessions and you have learned more about yourself and how you feel this has led you to realize that what you're working on is not helping you feel better. This can mean that the initial goal for counseling made sense at the time, but as you have dug deeper and understood more about yourself what you really need to work on has become clearer. What should follow then, as the focus shifts to working on a better goal, is that you should start to feel counseling is working— you may not feel 100 percent better but should feel you're headed in the right direction. If you're still left feeling counseling isn't working, it may make sense to revisit the goal again. Of course, it is not always the goal that may be the problem. Sometimes the approach taken when working toward a goal may need to be changed.

There are a multitude of different ways to approach the same concern or goal (see Questions 7–19 for more information on different types of therapy). Some are more problem or solution focused, whereas others are focused on helping the client develop insight. Problem- or solution-focused forms of counseling examine the nature of the concern. The client and counselor then work toward identifying a solution to the problem. This can be a trial-and-error endeavor. Even though the counselor likely knows what works for most people with the same or similar concerns, that particular solution may not work for you. Thus, the client and counselor discuss what did or did not work with that particular solution and then devise another solution for the client to try. Insight-oriented therapies are focused on helping the client understand why or how their concerns developed and may also spend time examining what is maintaining the problem; that is, what may be working to keep the problem in place despite the client's desire for and best efforts to make the problem go away. The idea with insight-oriented therapies is that as a client develops a greater understanding of their concern, they will be better equipped to identify, cope with, and prevent the problem from continuing or resurfacing in the future. Whatever type of counseling is used may not be a good fit for you as the client. The counselor may firmly believe that an insight-oriented approach is the way to go, but the way you think or your preferred way of approaching problems is to identify what the problem is and find a solution for it. Thus, an insight-oriented approach will feel very much like counseling is not working. The reverse is also true: if a client wants to better understand themselves and the problem but counseling is focused on identifying a specific solution, counseling will not feel it is working either. This brings us back to the recommendation of talking with the counselor about your concerns. You may not have the specific terms or language to describe why counseling isn't working, but an equally effective way of communicating what you need would be something like "I don't really want to figure out why this problem exists, I just want it gone" (problem/solution focused) or "I don't think you really understand me and what has created these problems to begin with. I would rather not brainstorm fixes for this quite yet" (insight oriented).

More often than not, when the client brings their concerns to the counselor even if it truly is simply "I don't feel like this is working," the counselor can work with the client to figure out what is not working and what might feel like a better route to take. Usually, this can be done effectively without changing counselors. Sometimes, however, the counselor may say something like "What you're asking for really makes a lot of sense and can be an effective approach to take. I do not, unfortunately, use that approach, and if we were to continue working together I think you would keep feeling like therapy isn't working which of course is not helpful for you. What I'd like to do is refer you to another counselor who does work in the way you are looking for. Would that be okay?" As a client you can certainly say "yes" or "no," or "I'm not sure" to something like that. In fact, you may want time to think about it or to take time in that session to talk more extensively with the counselor about what is the best decision for you.

Sometimes, of course, the issue isn't the goal or the type of therapy but is really more of a matter of fit (see Question 5 for more information about finding the right counselor). Your counselor may be highly skilled, but if your interactions with the counselor leave you feeling frustrated with how they interact with you (and it has nothing to do with taking an insight-oriented or solution-focused approach), then the issue is not their competence or the type of therapy they use but is more about a clash of personalities. In that case, it is a good idea to change course and find another counselor. If you don't feel comfortable in your sessions, then you will not be able to address what you need, which will undoubtedly leave you feeling therapy isn't working. It is also possible, however, that it is not a matter of fit but a matter of competence. Although professionals who diagnose and treat mental illness are highly trained, there are some, as there are in any profession, who may not be good at what they do. Thus, no matter how many times a goal is revisited or how many times you change how a particular goal is addressed, you will not feel better. You may even feel as if you like the counselor as a person but your work with them is not helping you. In either case it is truly best to cut ties with the counselor and find another one (see Question 35 on what to do if you don't like your counselor). As with all of the other factors covered for this question, it is usually best to talk as candidly as possible with the counselor. This is not, however, required, and if for any reason you would prefer to simply not go back, you have the right to do that unilaterally.

32. Are my sessions confidential?

The issue of confidentiality is a significant concern for most clients. Most clients want to know that what they share in their sessions with their counselor will not be repeated to anyone else. Generally, it is the case that what is said in the context of a client–counselor relationship is bound by the ethics and laws of confidentiality, meaning the counselor cannot share anything about your sessions (including the fact that you are meeting with the counselor) without your permission; however, there are some exceptions to this.

Most professional organizations that help regulate the practice of mental health professionals have a code of ethics that all of their members must adhere to. For example, members of the American Psychological Association (APA) follow a document called *The Ethical Principles of Psychologists and Code of Conduct*. This code has five general principles that include providing help and doing no harm; developing relationships based on trust; ensuring that their work is accurate, honest, and truthful; working with the notion of fairness and justice; and having a basic respect for the rights and dignity of all people. This code also describes specific ethical behavior, including, but not limited to, knowing one's boundaries of competence, how to ethically advertise services, record keeping, conducting research, and privacy and confidentiality. State laws created for the practice of mental health services are often based on a professional organization's code of ethics. For example, the laws that govern the practice of psychology in a particular state are likely based on the APA's Ethics Code, whereas the laws regulating the practice of counselors (see Question 3 for the differences between a counselor, therapist, psychologist, and psychiatrist) are likely based on the code of ethics created by the American Counseling Association. Regardless of the credentials of the counselor, the expectations around confidentiality tend to be the same: the professional cannot reveal anything about the work with a client to anyone else (including the fact that the client is working with the counselor) without the client's permission. There are, however, some important exceptions to this, which are referred to as the *limits of confidentiality*.

The limits of confidentiality have to do with whether the client is a threat to themselves or someone else. What this means is that if the counselor believes the client is actively suicidal or that they have made a specific threat of physical harm to a person or persons, then the counselor is both ethically and legally obligated to report that information to the appropriate people. If the client is suicidal, this may mean contacting a family member to let them know that the client may be suicidal and that the client should not be left alone for a specified period of time (e.g., until the next appointment when the client will be reassessed for safety). Sometimes the counselor may make the decision to call emergency services to have the client taken directly to a hospital with psychiatric services where the client would be formally evaluated and, if deemed necessary, admitted to the facility for their safety. If the client has made a specific threat of harm to a person or people, then the counselor is again ethically and legally obligated to report that threat to the legal authorities (e.g., the police) and to the person or people against whom the threat was made. These types of reports would be made regardless of the age of the client.

If the client is a minor, the procedures get a bit more complicated. In the case of children (but not adolescents), information in the session is still confidential, with the exceptions noted in the previous paragraph; however, the person(s) who would provide the permission about revealing session information to someone else would be the legal guardian(s) of the child. Thus, session information is not confidential from the legal guardians, but the legal guardians can determine if any information is to be shared with anyone else such as other family members, the child's pediatrician, and other health-care professionals. With regard to adolescents, the legal guardians are still legally responsible for their child and therefore have some legal rights to session information; however, depending on the state in which the mental health services are provided, there are some things discussed in the session that cannot be revealed to the legal guardians without the adolescent's permission. For example, on or after a particular age (e.g., 14 or 16 years old depending on state laws and the issue in question), the counselor cannot talk with legal guardians about session information related to drug or alcohol use, sexual activity, and so on. Although this is distressing to some guardians, the idea is that the adolescent needs to know they can talk about sensitive topics such as these without fear of reprisal from their legal guardians.

Regardless of the age of the client and who else may have a vested interest in the client's work with a counselor, the nature and limits to confidentiality must be made known to the client and/or their legal guardians. This is done at minimum via an informed consent document that would have been signed by the client and/or legal guardian prior to beginning counseling (see Questions 26 and 27 for more information about paperwork and the first session with a counselor). In addition, this information is often communicated verbally at the initial session, particularly the limits of confidentiality, to ensure that the client and/or legal guardians understand these limits and to address any questions or concerns any parties may have. It is acceptable for the client to ask questions about any situation they are particularly concerned about. For example, a 15-year-old may ask their counselor if the counselor has to tell their parents about drug use or sexual activity. This can always be done in terms of a hypothetical question such as "So, hypothetically if I told you I was drinking alcohol would you have to tell my parents?" or "Hypothetically, doc, if I told you I was having sex would you have to tell my grandma (assuming the grandmother is the legal guardian)?" Their answer will depend, in part, on the age of the client, the laws of the state in which they practice, and the counselor's way of handling sensitive behavior that may constitute a threat to the client. For example, if the adolescent is using a lot of drugs, driving while intoxicated, and having indiscriminant and unprotected sex, it may be possible for this to constitute a threat to one's self and therefore grounds for breaking confidentiality by telling the legal guardians about the client's behavior and the counselor's concerns about the behavior. It is impossible for a counselor to answer definitively "yes I would break confidentiality" or "no I would not break confidentiality" based on hypotheticals alone as there is often more revealed when the full situation is presented. What can happen, however, is that the counselor may become aware of when a client may be heading toward the limits of confidentiality and may literally stop the client to inform them in the moment that depending on what they say next the counselor may have to break confidentiality for the client's safety or the safety of someone else. This would then be discussed more fully, and the client would make the decision about whether they want to reveal anymore.

The issues surrounding confidentiality are, in many ways, straightforward and, in others, quite complex. Thus, it is important for the client to know as much as they can, via a discussion with their counselor, about how the counselor handles situations in which they may have to break confidentiality and thereby inform someone else about what the client has revealed in the session.

33. What does it mean if my counselor recommends psychological testing?

It is not uncommon for someone seeking assistance for mental health concerns to be referred to a psychologist for psychological testing. Ideally, whoever makes the referral will explain the purpose of the testing and why they are making the referral. Sometimes the referral is made by one's primary care provider (PCP), one's current counselor or therapist (see Question 3), or school personnel in the case of children and adolescents.

Generally, a referral for psychological testing means that there is a specific question you, a family member, a health-care provider, or someone in the school system has about your functioning. For example, you may have noticed that you often struggle in school in ways your peers do not, and you wonder if you have a learning disability (LD) or some other concern such as attention-deficit/hyperactivity disorder (ADHD). Another example might be that you have received medical and mental health treatment for quite some time but have not noticed much improvement. In this case, your counselor or PCP may recommend psychological testing to determine if there is something else going on that might explain your symptoms. This can mean that your current diagnosis may be incorrect or that your symptoms are such that they could reflect any number of mental health diagnoses, and completing psychological testing will help clarify what may be going on (see Question 22). This is important since one's diagnosis has a direct impact on what type of treatment may be recommended. Thus, if you are being treated for one diagnosis but psychological testing reveals that there is another diagnosis that better explains your symptoms, then treatment can be adjusted. Psychological testing is not required to render a diagnosis; however, when one's mental health experiences are complex, formal testing can help illuminate for both you and your mental health treatment provider what may explain the complexity and ultimately ensure you receive the appropriate treatment.

The assessments included as part of one's psychological testing will vary, in part, on the psychologist conducting the testing but will be primarily dictated by the nature of the question or concern. For example, if there is a question about a patient's diagnosis, formal assessments may include a symptom checklist or a paper-and-pencil test specifically designed to identify the diagnosis. When someone is referred for an LD or other concern about intellectual functioning, the assessments will likely include an IQ test and an achievement test. There are specific tests for infants, children, and adults, which means that the age of the person being tested will also affect which assessments are used. Other assessments include personality tests, neuropsychological tests, work-related or disability tests, and behavioral assessments. It should be expected that whatever formal tests are used to complete one's psychological testing, there will also be a clinical interview. This type of interview involves the person conducting the psychological assessment asking a series of questions designed to gather background information and to gain your perspective on what is going on and how your symptoms are affecting you. Sometimes family members, teachers, or other people who may have important information to share are interviewed or asked to complete paper-and-pencil tests based on their understanding of your symptoms. This is particularly relevant, for example, when there is a concern about something like ADHD or other diagnoses that affect children.

Ultimately, once the clinical interview and all assessments are conducted, the psychologist who completed the assessment will write up a formal report summarizing your history to date, your symptoms, your (and/or others') understanding of your symptoms and how they affect you, the results of each assessment that was completed (e.g., summary of your IQ results, summary of your achievement test results), a summary of what all the results mean, and a list of recommendations based on the results as well as the areas of your life that are impacted by your symptoms (e.g., recommendations for taking tests in a school setting). The report is typically sent to the referring health-care provider or school personnel (assuming they have permission to receive the results; see Question 26), to the patient or their legal guardian, and anyone else who may need to know about the results and has permission to receive the results (e.g., PCP).

One final note. Psychological testing is a different service compared to counseling or psychotherapy. As such, your health insurance plan (see Questions 40–44) may cover therapy services differently than it covers psychological testing. Thus, it is always important to contact your health insurance company to find out how much your insurance will pay for psychological testing.

34. What does it mean if my counselor recommends medication?

Medications prescribed for psychological disorders are known as psychotropic medications. These are medications prescribed for the purpose of helping someone manage symptoms related to their mental health diagnosis. Different types of psychotropic medications include stimulants, antidepressants, antipsychotics, mood stabilizers, and antianxiety medications (i.e., anxiolytics).

Typically, medications are developed and marketed for a specific disorder (e.g., major depressive disorder, bipolar disorder); however, many medications can be used to treat more than one disorder. Sometimes there is enough scientific research to indicate that a specific medication is known to be effective in the treatment of more than one disorder. In other cases some medications are prescribed for disorders "off label," which means the medication is not officially known to treat that disorder but enough clinicians have had experience with it to know how the drug may affect various mental health symptoms. Whenever you or someone you care about is prescribed a particular medication, it is a good idea and is perfectly acceptable to ask specifically about what the drug is prescribed for, what symptoms is it supposed to target, how soon you should notice results if the medication is working as expected, and what side effects are common.

Regardless of any medication that may or may not be prescribed, it is not uncommon for people to question why a medication may be needed in the first place. Some patients are opposed to taking medication, in part, because they don't want to have to rely on a chemical to make them feel better. They may also have known someone who has taken a medication for mental illness that seemingly made the person feel worse and therefore they don't want to go through the same thing. Still others may have the perspective that taking a medication for a mental health issue means they are "really crazy" and, therefore, if their counselor recommends a referral for medication, their counselor thinks their problems are really bad and that there is no way they can get better without taking a medication. Some may also be concerned about becoming addicted to prescription medications. While it is true that some psychotropic medications can be addictive, many are not; however, just as with most situations, once a substance of any kind is introduced over time, the body and brain get used to the medication. This is why stopping any medication "cold turkey" is not recommended since the body and brain need to slowly get used to no longer having the medication in the system.

In some cases, it may be true that taking a medication in addition to working with a counselor is the standard of care, thus indicating that in order to feel much better medication may be strongly recommended. In many cases, medication is often recommended either when counseling alone has made no impact on problematic symptoms or when only minimal impact has been made. In those cases, medication is recommended to help alleviate symptoms enough so that counseling can be more effective. Sometimes symptoms can be significant enough that the individual needs even a slight reduction in symptoms so that they can engage more effectively in therapy. For example, someone who deals with regular feelings of anxiety may be so filled with anxiety during counseling sessions that they are unable to fully process and follow through on recommendations their counselor made. This may occur not because the patient is incapable of doing whatever was recommended but because they were unable to focus enough to fully process what was being asked of them. Thus, taking an antianxiety medication may be recommended so that the patient's anxiety symptoms can be low enough to more fully engage in therapy.

As noted earlier in this answer, taking a medication or not is always up to the person for whom the prescription is written (or their legal guardians). Thus, if a counselor recommends a referral to a psychiatrist or other clinician who can prescribe psychotropic medications, that does not mean a patient must take whatever is prescribed. Before deciding, however, it is critical that the patient (and/or legal guardians) understand what the medication will and will not do for them, and what could happen if they do not take the medication. Some clinicians are certainly more likely to recommend medication and to impress upon their patients why it is important to take a medication. When this occurs, the clinician is more than likely operating from a position of offering all possible solutions to help get their patient to where the patient wants to be.

35. I don't like my therapist—what should I do?

You have finally decided to schedule an appointment with a counselor. You've done your homework on finding a counselor who accepts your health insurance (see Questions 40–44) and who treats the symptoms that you are dealing with, and you've even heard from others that this particular counselor is good (see Question 5). After meeting with the counselor the first time, you realized you didn't feel entirely comfortable but chalked that up to having just met them and being in the early stages of getting to know one another. After a few more meetings you realize that you don't really like your counselor. It isn't that they are mean or even that they don't seem to care. It simply does not feel "right" to you and that you aren't getting the help you need.

It is not that unusual to determine that you do not like your counselor for one reason or another; however, before discontinuing work with this counselor in favor of trying another, it is useful to contemplate if the reason you don't like this counselor may be a reason you might not like any counselor (e.g., they aren't giving you "the" answers to your concerns). If you feel fairly confident that your dislike for or discomfort with the counselor is not related to something that is more about you than them, then it is worth seeing if you can figure out why things don't feel right. This can help clarify for you what is going on and can also help you communicate to your counselor what is not going well about the counseling.

Sometimes what is unlikeable about a counselor is their approach to working with clients. Many counselors are flexible and are able to work with their clients in a variety of ways. For example, they may be able to help you explore why your symptoms exist if you want to develop that kind of understanding of yourself (e.g., psychodynamic psychotherapy; see Question 8), or they may be more solution focused (e.g., cognitive behavioral therapy; see Question 11), which means they will work with you to identify the specific things you don't like and identify specific steps you can take to make changes. If you had hoped for one approach but got another, fixing the relationship may be as simple as letting your therapist know that you'd prefer to work more concretely on your problems (e.g., solution focused) or to explore more about why your concerns keep resurfacing for you (e.g., insight oriented). Either way you may find that your counselor is able to adapt to your request and that how the relationship feels improves to the point that you are able to work effectively with your therapist. If your therapist is unable to accommodate your request for a change in approach, there is a really good chance that the therapist can recommend someone who works the way you would like and can provide that referral for you.

Sometimes your feelings about your counselor have nothing to do with how they go about their work with you but have more to do with who they are as a person. You may not like their communication style, their non-verbals (e.g., facial expressions, tone of voice), or something else about them just does not "click" for you. In this case, as with their approach to working with you, the issue is one of fit. Changing one's approach, as noted in the previous paragraph, may be easy for them or may be solved by a referral to another counselor, and in that case the issue of fit is resolved. If, however, the poor fit has to do with how the two of you interact with one another, then the change needed may, in fact, be a different counselor. If this is the conclusion you have come to, there is more than one way of handling this.

It is acceptable to simply not schedule another appointment. This is preferred to not showing up for a scheduled appointment or not calling to cancel when you realize you don't intend to keep the appointment. Although nothing bad will happen to you if you don't show up (the counselor may, however, have a cancelation policy that makes you responsible for the entire cost of the session), it is a courtesy to the counselor to let them know as soon as possible if you will not be keeping your appointment so that they can schedule another patient at that time. You do not have to provide a reason for why you are not keeping the appointment if you do not want to, and you can say something like "I'll call again later if I'd like to schedule another appointment in the future."

Another approach to ending a therapy relationship is to keep your next appointment and to start it by letting the counselor know that you do not think that the therapy relationship is a good fit for you at this time. This can be a scary thing to do because admitting you don't like someone, or that you do not like their approach to helping you, can make you feel quite vulnerable. Most counselors will talk with you professionally and respectfully about what it is that is not working for you and whether there is anything they can do differently that may change how things feel for you and ultimately help you talk through what kind of counselor you think would be a good fit (if you know) so that he or she can make a referral for you. An additional reason for taking the time and interpersonal risk of ending a therapy relationship in this way is the opportunity to say goodbye and to end the relationship in a way that feels good to you. We do not often have an opportunity to have the kind of goodbye that feels good, and this is one of them. Being able to say what you need, thanking them for the help they did provide (even if the only thing that felt helpful was the referral), and leaving with the feeling that it was OK for saying what you needed to say will help you feel good about yourself.

One of the most important elements of counseling and therapy is that the relationship between you and your counselor feels good enough to you so that you get what you need—ultimately that is what the therapy relationship is for. Therefore, if you need to end the relationship because you don't like your counselor even if you don't know why, it is within your right to do so and will ultimately be beneficial for you in the long run since you'll be able to find another counselor who is a better fit.

36. What is **HIPAA** and how does it affect me?

HIPAA is the Health Insurance Portability and Accountability Act and was enacted in 1996 by the federal government. The purpose of the act was, and continues to be, to ensure the continuity of health insurance coverage, the prevention of excessive spending and fraud in the use of health insurance, people have access to insurance coverage for long-term care services, and to encourage companies and individuals to use medical savings accounts [a.k.a. health savings accounts (HSA) or health reimbursement arrangement (HRA)], and so on. Thus, HIPAA helps to ensure health-care coverage for people when they change or lose their job, establishes standards for electronic health-care records and how they are shared, determines how medical spending accounts can be used tax free, establishes rules for group health plans, and regulates life insurance policies that are owned by companies.

Practically, HIPAA gives individuals and their families more say with regard to how their health information is used. This includes how the information is stored, with whom the information is shared, and how the information is shared with others. The policies associated with HIPAA help to ensure that one's health information remains protected and private. If one's rights are violated under the HIPAA guidelines, those who improperly stored or shared protected health information can be held accountable either civilly or criminally depending on the nature of the violation. HIPAA does allow for the sharing of health information, even if you don't want the information shared, in order to protect public health. For example, if you have a communicable disease that can easily spread to others, you likely will have no say with regard to how and with whom your health information related to this issue is shared. Generally, if you or something about you (e.g., the communicable disease you contracted) is a "serious and imminent threat" to others (e.g., abuse or neglect, domestic violence), then HIPAA can be ethically and legally violated and your relevant health information shared to appropriate persons and authorities. Other reasons a health-care provider can violate HIPAA include (but are not limited to) complying with a court order or subpoena; helping to identify a suspect, fugitive, or witness; and reporting on the death of someone. Outside of situations like this, you have to provide written permission in order for your health information to be shared (see Questions 26 and 32).

Most health-care providers and offices require you to sign a form stating that you understand your rights under this federal privacy act. In addition, by seeking services from a health-care provider or agency, you were likely made aware of the fact that using health insurance means that certain information must be shared with your insurance company in order for claims to be filed and payment to be rendered to the provider. Details about your treatment are not typically shared with insurance companies unless they require a rationale for why continued services are necessary. Usually what is shared with insurance companies is your diagnosis and the type of service provided. For example, insurance companies pay differently for individual therapy, couples counseling, group therapy (see Question 20), and whether the treatment is conducted on an inpatient or outpatient basis (see Question 21). Thus, in addition to your diagnosis, your treatment provider will submit a code to the insurance company indicating the type of service provided. Whenever health information must be shared or even when permission is granted for a health-care provider to share information, HIPAA denotes that only the minimum information necessary to reasonably communicate should be released to a third party (i.e., someone or an agency other than the provider or agency for which they work and someone other than the person receiving the services).

HIPAA also indicates that you (or your family if you are a minor) have the right to see your health records and to receive a copy of them should you make such request. Whatever is included in your health record should not be kept from you. Permission to share any portion of your health record with someone else can be provided by you (or your legal guardian) in writing, verbally if you are present at the time and do not object to sharing the information, or the provider determines it is in your best interest to share the information even if you are not present and thus have not explicitly granted permission for them to share the information. Thus, while consumers have significant rights to their health records and how information is shared, their privacy is not absolute. As with most aspects related to your health care, it is always a good idea to ask questions about what health-related information you have given permission to your provider to share and with whom and under what circumstances might your health-care provider share your health information without your explicit permission (see also Question 32).

37. What if I don't want to go to counseling—can anyone make me go?

The short answer to this question, for most situations, is "no." The longer answer is a bit more complicated. Just as there is for most things, there are always exceptions to the simple answer. The reason the short answer to this question is "no" has to do with the idea that counseling is rarely mandated and generally works best when the patient wants to receive counseling services and therefore is voluntarily seeking this type of help. What follows is a discussion of the situations in which you can be forced to receive counseling or mental health services.

When you are an adult, one situation in which someone can make you go to counseling is if you are mandated by court order to receive counseling. This occurs when you have had some legal problems (e.g., violent behavior) and you are either ordered or agree in a plea arrangement to seek counseling for the issues that got you into trouble with the law in the first place. Outside of a court order under such circumstances, another situation in which someone may be mandated to receive mental health services would be if you are deemed to be a danger to yourself or someone else. Making you receive services under these circumstances, however, usually involves the legal system whereby a judge will hear testimony from a psychologist or physician who will make a case for why you are an imminent threat to yourself or someone else and thus need mental health services immediately whether you want them or not. Other situations in which an adult may be compelled (although not necessarily forced) to receive mental health services might come from an employer, a spouse, or someone else who tells you that you need to get counseling or other mental health services or some consequence, usually negative, will occur. For example, a spouse may tell you that unless you get psychological help they will divorce you, or an employer may say that unless you get mental health services for something that is keeping you from performing your job adequately you will be fired. There are, of course, laws that regulate under which circumstances, for example, an employer can actually terminate your employment if it relates to a mental health issue. Nonetheless, under these and similar circumstances it may feel like you are forced to go to counseling; however, you do have a choice in the matter. The reality is, however, that if you choose not to seek services then you may not be able to avoid a negative outcome such as getting fired or getting a divorce.

When you are a minor child or adolescent, you may or may not be mandated by a court of law to seek counseling; however, your parents or legal guardians may insist that you seek counseling for something they think you need help with. You can, of course, refuse to go; however, parents often have the power to insist and to enforce consequences (e.g., losing car privileges or computer privileges) should you refuse to go. Similar to the situations noted with adults, the alternative to going to counseling may be persuasive enough that it can feel like you have to go and that your parents are making you go. In some situations, schools may insist that in order to remain a student at their institution you have to seek mental health services for whatever behavior is interfering with your ability to behave appropriately at school.

Even the situations in which it can feel as if someone is making you go to counseling, in most situations, you don't have to; however, the alternative may feel worse, so going to counseling may seem like something you're willing to do in order to keep whatever privileges you have or to avoid a negative consequence. Regardless of whether or not you are court ordered to attend counseling or are in any other way compelled to go, there are still regulations with respect to confidentiality, which means that what you talk about may or may not be shared with those who mandated or insisted you seek counseling (see Question 32).

38. What should I do if my family/friends make fun of me for going to therapy?

Ideally, of course, your family and friends are not making fun of you or in any other way giving you a hard time for going to a counselor or therapist. If they are, however, there is a good chance they are doing so because they are misinformed about how counseling can be beneficial and they may hold some outdated opinions about who goes to see a counselor (e.g., only "crazy" people see a counselor). You may be able to let negative comments or attitudes about counseling roll off your back; however, for those who are negatively affected by less-than supportive friends or family, there are some things that you can do, none of which are guaranteed to change their mind or to get them to stop making fun of you but will help you continue with what you know is best for you regardless of what other people think.

It is, unfortunately, not that uncommon for patients to get the third degree from friends or family members who have no familiarity with mental health services or who hold the opinion that only a certain type of person needs that kind of help. Thus, their questions or statements likely revolve around trying to figure out if you are "that kind of person." Some patients know that their family or friends will not understand why someone would seek counseling if they are not crazy, and therefore, these clients do not tell these friends and family that they are working with a counselor. Moreover, it is not uncommon for people to think that seeing a counselor means you're "weak" and that "all you have to do is pull yourself up by your bootstraps and get over it." Such statements or opinions reflect an ignorant (i.e., uninformed) point of view and one that does not leave room for another way of handling one's struggles. Thus, one way to deal with friends and family who are making fun of you for going to therapy is to not tell them. You may know enough about them that not telling them in the first place is the best course of action. If you have already told them, however, and they make jokes about it or make snide comments, then another course of action is to stop talking about your counseling with these people. If they ask whether you're still seeing your headshrinker or if you are "still a basket case," you can simply say "yes" (even though you aren't a basket case) and change the subject, or you can say something like "I'm not comfortable talking about that right now/with you."

Another approach you can take is to educate them. You can tell them that most people can benefit from working with someone whose job it is to listen in a nonjudgmental way and to help you become the best version of yourself possible. In addition, you can tell them that not all people who seek counseling or therapy have a mental health diagnosis, and although most do, it does not mean they are crazy or a basket case or whatever term they may use to malign anyone seeking this type of support. You can tell them that most people who see a counselor feel better. Some feel better right away and continue to see their counselor to prevent their symptoms from coming back or to simply improve their lives as much as possible. You can also try to educate friends or family who do not understand why you're seeing a counselor by using an analogy. You can say that taking care of one's mental health is no different than taking care of one's physical health, and since the mind and body are connected there is a good chance that by seeing a counselor you are also taking care of your overall health. You can also say that going to see a counselor when you are not feeling well is no different than seeing your primary care provider when you feel sick. You need someone with training and expertise to help figure out what is going on and what the best course of treatment is or what help is recommended. If none of these approaches work, or if you'd prefer a different and more direct route, you can say something like "I appreciate that you don't think counseling is useful but I do and I'd appreciate it if you would not make fun of me for doing something I know is helping me." Such a statement is direct but respectful. Nonetheless, it can be heard by others as a direct challenge or confrontation, and they may, as a result, respond in a way that makes it clear they do not care about your opinion or that you are trying to help yourself. They may, therefore, take your comment as an attack and attack back. In such situations the best course of action may be to change the subject or to literally walk away.

Unfortunately, those who make fun of you or anyone else for seeking mental health services may not be interested in your thoughts and opinions, or facts related to how much these types of services can help. Ultimately, whatever you do in a situation like this is whatever you think will work best for you, but there is no reason you have to listen to anyone, no matter who it is, make fun of a choice you made, particularly one related to your well-being.

39. How can I encourage someone who is struggling to seek counseling?

There is no doubt that seeing someone you care about struggling with any kind of problem is difficult, especially if whatever they're dealing with has been going on for a long time (see Question 1 for more information on figuring out when to seek counseling). It can also be difficult to know the best way to support someone under these circumstances. It is certainly possible that all your friend or family member needs, temporarily, is time or a shoulder to lean on. However, when their problems or concerns seem to persist or they are looking for more from you than you are comfortable giving or are able to give, it may be a good idea to recommend your friend or family member seek counseling.

Encouraging someone to seek counseling may be as simple as asking them if they are seeing a counselor or if they would consider seeing a counselor. If they are open to the idea, there is a good chance they are already in counseling with someone, or they may say that they agree it would be a good idea to see a professional (see Question 3 for more information on the different types of professionals). In this case it can be helpful to have a list of names and phone numbers to give to your friend or family member. Many people find a counselor or therapist by word of mouth, so if you have worked with a counselor or therapist yourself, or if someone else you know has mentioned that they like their counselor or therapist, then these would be good names to include on your list. If you do not have or are not comfortable creating such a list (no matter how formal or informal), you can encourage your friend or family member to seek a counselor who may be available to them through their employer or school. If such services do not exist, then contacting the employer's human resources department or the school's student services center (or school counselor for K-12 students) should result in receiving a list of names of counselors in the area. In addition, if your friend or family member has health insurance, there is a good chance that mental health services are covered by their policy (though this is not always the case) and their insurance company's website likely has an option to search for a provider (see Questions 40–44 for more information on insurance).

The more complicated situations involving encouraging someone you care about to seek mental health services usually revolve around those who do not believe they need help and those who are, for one reason or another, against the idea of counseling or therapy. It is possible that they believe only those who are severely mentally ill (i.e., those who need to be hospitalized) need counseling or therapy. Of course, anyone who is struggling with a mental health issue, no matter how serious, can benefit from working with a trained mental health professional. Sometimes encouraging your friend or family member may be a matter of providing this kind of education: most people can benefit from mental health services, and seeking counseling or therapy does not mean there is something fundamentally wrong with you. Another concern many people have is that they will be personally judged by anyone who hears about what they are struggling with. You can encourage them by saying you're not judging them (only if this is true, of course) and that mental health professionals are explicitly educated and trained to not judge someone but to help them in whatever way they need help. When push comes to shove, sometimes all you can do is to be a broken record by saying that you care about your friend or family member, you're worried about them, and you really think they would benefit from talking with someone who is trained to help with what they're dealing with.

If you are trying to encourage someone who is reluctant to seek professional help, you can offer to go with them to their counseling appointment. This can mean you travel with them to the counselor's office and wait in the waiting room until the session is over, or it can mean that you offer to sit in on the session with them. This is usually acceptable to most professionals; however, at some point the counselor or therapist will likely say that the sessions should only have the counselor and patient present. If your friend or family member refuses, again, many professionals may allow you to continue to sit in for moral support; however, it is often the case that patients are not as candid as they need to be when another person is in the room, no matter how supportive or nonjudgmental that person is. Therefore, you can offer to move to the waiting room and indicate that you'll be there for them if needed. Sitting in on sessions may be more than you are comfortable with, and you would be under no obligation to take this route. It is, however, a possible option if both you and your friend or family member are comfortable with it.

Insurance and Paying for Therapy

40. How much does therapy cost?

The cost of therapy is not universal due to the fact that there are many factors involved in what a particular counselor or therapist might charge. Those factors include what their degree and license are, whether they take insurance (see Question 41 for more information about whether you need health insurance to pay for counseling), where in the country they are located, whether they have a unique specialty (see Question 23 for more information about specialties), and what type of service is provided.

Generally, a licensed mental health professional has a graduate degree of some kind such as a master's degree, a doctoral degree, or a medical degree (see Questions 3 and 4 for more information about differences between professionals). Professionals with the highest medical degrees (e.g., MD, DO) tend to charge more than those with any other degree, including those with a doctoral degree (i.e., PhD or PsyD). Those with a PhD or PsyD tend to charge more than those with a master's degree (e.g., MS, MSW) and those with other medical degrees such as those in nursing; however, some nurses may make more than doctoral-level practitioners depending on what they are licensed to do. For example, a professional providing counseling and psychotherapy services is going to earn more if they have a doctoral or the highest medical degree; however, if the professional also prescribes medication, then they may be able to charge more than a professional who does not prescribe medication. Usually medical professionals are the only ones who can prescribe medication, although in some states licensed psychologists can prescribe medications with additional training and supervision.

Insurance coverage for mental health services is also a factor in terms of what therapy will cost. Whether a professional accepts insurance for mental health services is somewhat complicated with respect to how much it may cost to have a session with them. Some professionals do not take insurance but offer services at an adjusted rate or on a sliding scale (i.e., what you pay is based on your income) because they assume most people cannot afford their full fee, whereas others who do not take insurance charge their full fee and thus only take on clients who can afford it. Those who accept insurance will have their per session rates set by each insurance company. Insurance companies set session rates based on the type of degree and license a professional has—those with higher degrees usually have higher rates than those with lower degrees. For example, an insurance company may agree to a rate of $125 per session for psychiatrists (MD degree), $110 per session for psychologists (e.g., PhD or PsyD degree), and $80 for master's-level practitioners (e.g., MS or MSW).

It may seem strange that the location of the mental health practitioner will impact how much is charged; however, most readers who have traveled know that food and gas are more or less expensive depending on what part of the country you're in. This is due, in part, to local taxes, supply and demand, cost of living, and so on. Wherever the cost of living is higher, such as large metropolitan areas and certain regions of the United States, what a counselor or therapist charges for their services will be higher than those with the exact training and credentials as a professional who lives elsewhere. Thus, where you live and where you receive mental health services do affect how much therapy may cost.

Another factor that may affect the cost of counseling and therapy is whether the counselor or therapist has a unique or a high-demand specialty. This, too, can vary from state to state or from one region of the country to another. Thus, it is not possible to say which specialties or services may be scarcer or in higher demand overall. One way to determine this for where you live would be via word of mouth (i.e., asking friends, family, or coworkers what they know about mental health specialists in the area) or to ask another health-care provider like one's primary care practitioner. If you need a particular specialty for you or a family member (e.g., child psychologist or psychiatrist, eating disorder specialist, forensic psychologist) and there aren't many in your area, you may pay more for their services.

Another factor that affects how much counseling and therapy costs has to do with what type of service is provided (see Question 33 for more information about psychological testing and Question 34 for more information about psychiatric medications). With regard to the cost of sessions, usually the initial session costs more than any regularly scheduled sessions after that. The reasons for this can include the fact that the initial session is longer than all following sessions (see Question 27 for more information about the first session), and/or more paperwork is required to document why someone is seeking counseling or therapy, what their history and their family's history with mental illness are, whether they are taking any medications, and so on (see Question 25 for more information about the initial paperwork). In addition to the initial session costing more than the sessions that follow, there are other instances in which there might be a higher fee. These include having a crisis session (i.e., a nonscheduled session, usually before your next regularly scheduled appointment, that is needed because of increased, acute distress), couples or family therapy (see Question 20 for more information on these and other therapies), and a session that is more than 45–50 minutes which is the standard session length for counseling or therapy.

Finally, and as discussed more fully in Questions 41, 42, and 44, what you personally pay for a counseling or therapy session will depend on whether you have health insurance that covers mental health services, if you have a deductible, and if you are required to pay a co-payment at each session.

41. Do I need health insurance to see a counselor? What kinds of health insurance are there? How do I get insurance?

You do not need health insurance to see a counselor or therapist; however, many people may not be able to afford counseling sessions without having insurance. Many mental health practitioners charge $100 or more per session, and in some regions of the country the cost can be as high as $200 or $300 per session; however, as will be discussed, if you have insurance that covers mental health services, you will likely not pay that amount yourself.

Health insurance that covers mental health services usually works the same as it does for routine checkups with your primary care provider, having a specific medical procedure done, and so on. If you have health insurance, you probably know that you do not pay for the entire service yourself. You pay part and your insurance company pays part. How much is paid to the professional providing the service is set by the insurance company and is usually less than the provider's usual and customary rate. What that means is that without insurance a counselor may charge $100, which would be their usual and customary rate; however, if that counselor agrees to accept a particular insurance, they will enter into a contract with that insurance company binding the provider to the rate that the insurance company states is reasonable for that provider's service. That amount is always less than the provider's usual and customary rate. Each insurance company sets their own rates, so one insurance company may say the same service is worth $80 and another may say it is worth $95. Either way, the provider agrees that they will be paid only for the amount they agree on with the insurance company. As the client you will pay for a portion of that agreed-on amount, or you may pay the entire amount (see Question 44 for more information on why an insurance company may not pay for counseling or therapy). If your health insurance covers mental health benefits, it is highly likely that you will not pay the entire amount. Typically, you will be responsible for a co-payment or a coinsurance (see Question 42 for more information about these and other insurance-related terminology), which is either a set amount (e.g., $25 per session) or a percentage (e.g., 15% of the session fee), and the insurance company pays the rest. Some insurance plans, however, have a deductible, which means you will have to pay the full amount until you have met your deductible (see Question 42 for more information about deductibles).

With regard to the kinds of insurance there are, this gets a bit more complicated. Most employers offer health insurance, but not all health insurance plans cover mental health services. In addition, not all employers are required to offer health insurance. Employers that offer health insurance offer what is often referred to as private insurance. These are companies that are not subsidized by the state or federal government. Individuals can also purchase insurance directly from a private company, but it tends to be more costly than getting it through one's employer as employer-subsidized insurance means that your employer will pay for part of your monthly or bimonthly premium (see Question 42 for more information on this and other insurance-related terms). Medicare and Medicaid are government-subsidized insurances, which usually means there is little to no cost for having these insurances or for seeing health-care providers. Medicare and Medicaid are offered at the state and federal levels; however, not just anyone can get these types of insurances. You must meet strict criteria based on your age, the number of dependents you have, your annual income, and whether you have a documented disability.

Specifics about your particular insurance, including whether mental health services are covered and if you have a deductible, are best asked of your human resources department through your job if you have the insurance through your employer, and/or of the insurance company itself.

42. What do insurance-related terms like "in-network," "out-of-network," "deductible," "co-payment," and "coinsurance" mean?

There are a variety of insurance-related terms that are important to know about and understand when not only picking the type of insurance you want but also when seeking services from a health-care provider. The terms discussed here include insurance card, insurance premium, deductible, co-payment, coinsurance, usual reasonable and customary, out-of-pocket, in-network, out-of-network, covered services, and preexisting condition.

Once you purchase an insurance plan (from your employer, from the government, or directly from a private insurance company), you will receive an insurance card from the insurance company. If you have any dependents or a legal partner (e.g., you are married or have a legal union), each of you will have your own insurance card. This is because dollar amounts spent on services are tracked by each individual covered under the plan. The insurance card has your name (or the name of your dependent), the type of insurance plan you have (e.g., HMO, PPO), your insurance ID number, a group number identifying your employer (if applicable), a series of dollar amounts or percentages indicating co-payment or coinsurance amounts, what you are responsible for if you seek emergency services from a hospital, and on the back of the card contact information for you or your provider to call if you have questions about a service.

"Insurance premium" refers to how much it costs to have insurance. This does not include what it costs for health-care services (i.e., when you see a physician for a checkup or a counselor for therapy sessions). The insurance premium is reflected in a monthly or bimonthly payment you make to the insurance company directly or through your employer. If you pay your insurance premium directly to an insurance company, it is likely that you are paying for the insurance on your own and no other entity (i.e., your employer or the government) is sharing the cost with you. If you have your insurance through your employer, they likely pay for part of your insurance premium and you pay for the remainder. Many employers allow you to have your portion of the insurance premium automatically deducted from your paycheck.

A "deductible" refers to an amount of money you have to pay for services before the insurance company starts to pay for a portion of or all of a service you need. A deductible can be a few hundred dollars to several thousand dollars. Usually the higher the deductible (e.g., several thousand dollars), the smaller your insurance premium, and the smaller the deductible (e.g., a few hundred dollars), the larger the insurance premium. Once you have met your deductible, the insurance will start paying for some or all of the cost of your services. Not all insurance plans have a deductible, which means you will pay only for a portion of the service as long as it is covered (see covered services in the following paragraphs) by your insurance plan. Deductibles are often set based on the individual family member and for the family as a whole, and they restart each year, which is based on either the calendar year or the day and month your insurance plan began.

When your deductible is met, or if your insurance plan does not have a deductible, then you pay a co-payment or a coinsurance when you receive a covered service for a health-care provider. A co-payment is a set dollar amount (e.g., $10, $25, $40) that you are responsible for. The dollar amount is set by the insurance company and may be different depending on the plan you choose. That is, if you want to see a counselor for therapy, your co-payment for one insurance plan may be $10 but for another insurance plan it may be $25. Usually the dollar amount(s) for the co-payment(s) for regular health-care services is printed on the insurance card you receive from the insurance company. If more than one dollar amount is listed on the card, it usually means that you may pay a larger co-payment for specialist services or specific types of prescribed medications. Your insurance company will have information about what type of provider is considered a specialist and which medications may require a larger co-payment. Alternatively, instead of a specific dollar amount, you may see a percentage or list of percentages. These percentages represent your coinsurance. Instead of paying $10 for a service, you may be responsible for 10 percent of what the service or prescription costs. If there is more than one percentage listed on the card, it usually means different types of services and/or medications require you to pay a larger or smaller percentage of the cost. Whatever percentage you are responsible for, the insurance company pays the remaining percentage.

As noted here and in Question 40, the cost of a service is set by the insurance company, and it usually sets the cost for a service based on what is usual, reasonable, and customary for that specific service, by similar providers, and based on the geographical area where the services are performed. In a rural area of a state, the usual, reasonable, and customary cost may be $100, whereas in an urban area of the same state, the usual, reasonable, and customary cost may be $200.

"Out-of-pocket expenses" refers to what you pay as opposed to what the insurance company pays. Sometimes health-care providers will indicate that a service is not covered by your insurance or that you have a large deductible and therefore you need to pay for the service out-of-pocket. This can certainly add up; however, many insurance plans have an out-of-pocket maximum. This means that once you have paid a certain dollar amount (often in thousands of dollars), you will no longer have to pay for any covered medical expense for the remainder of your plan year. Many plans have an out-of-pocket maximum for each individual covered under the plan and for the entire family. For example, if your child had a lot of medical expenses and whatever you paid for those services met the out-of-pocket maximum for that child, then any covered services that child receives the rest of the year will be paid 100 percent by the insurance company. The remainder of the family will still continue to pay as normal until their out-of-pocket maximum is met or the entire family's out-of-pocket maximum is met. If the family's limit is met, then no one on that insurance plan will pay anything for covered services for the rest of the plan year.

When considering which health-care provider you may want to see for counseling services, it is important to consider if that provider is in-network or out-of-network. In-network means the provider takes your insurance, which usually means you will have lower co-payment or coinsurance than if you were to see a provider that is out-of-network for the same service. An out-of-network provider is someone who does not take your insurance. This does not mean that you cannot see this provider for the service you need, but it will likely mean that you will pay a higher co-payment or coinsurance. In some cases, it may mean that you are responsible for the entire amount of the service. That is, the insurance will not pay any of the service, even if the service is a covered service on your plan, because you have an out-of-network provider. Finding out what your in-network and out-of-network benefits are for the service you need is important prior to setting up an appointment. Having this information can help you avoid billing surprises after you have already received the service.

"Medically necessary treatment" is a term that can be used to determine whether a particular service will be covered. The term refers to health-care services that are intended to prevent or treat a condition according to accepted standards of care. In the context of counseling and therapy, this may mean that the insurance company determines that a certain number of sessions is all that is necessary to treat or prevent a particular mental health diagnosis. The insurance company may also determine that only specific methods of treatment (e.g., cognitive behavioral therapy, interpersonal psychotherapy; see Questions 7–19) should be used with a particular mental health diagnosis. Thus, if your therapist is using a different form of treatment than they recommend, it is possible that they will not cover any portion of the cost of your sessions. Your counselor or therapist can work with the insurance company to establish whether the treatment he or she provides, including the number of sessions, is medically necessary.

An "insurance claim" refers to the request by you or your counselor for the insurance company to cover a particular service. There are specific procedures, forms, and information required in order for a claim to be processed. Many counselors will submit claims on your behalf, providing the insurance company with all of the requisite information for the service to be covered. If, however, your counselor does not take insurance, you would need to submit the claim to the insurance company yourself. Your counselor should, however, be able to give you the information you need (e.g., the diagnosis code, the procedure code), but your counselor will not necessarily know in what form your insurance company requires the information. For example, you may be able to submit the information online through its website. Or you may need to submit the information in writing on a form or in a letter. This is something your insurance company can tell you along with exactly what information you need to include when you submit the claim.

43. Do I have to get a special authorization to see a therapist?

Whether you need to get a special authorization to see a therapist depends on the insurance company as well as the plan you have. Some of this is regulated by state and federal laws, but you don't necessarily need to know what the laws are, simply what your insurance plan requires.

Many insurance companies approach seeing a counselor or therapist the same as if you were seeing your primary care provider (PCP) for routine checkups. You don't need a special authorization to see your PCP for your annual physical and some other standard services (e.g., health screenings, flu shots), and you therefore would not need an authorization for routine counseling. If you need an authorization for mental health treatment, sometimes your PCP needs to formally refer you for mental health treatment and will inform your insurance company that they have done so. You will receive a letter from your insurance company stating that the service has been approved (i.e., authorized) and will indicate how long the approval lasts and may specify how many sessions you are approved for. The specific number of sessions allowed may be as low as 3 sessions or as high as 52 (roughly one session per week for the entire year). Other insurance plans may not require that your PCP make a formal referral, but you still need to get an authorization from the insurance company for mental health sessions.

Not getting the authorization can mean that even if the service is covered by your insurance plan, the insurance company will not pay for any part of the service because you did not get their approval first. The good news is that many, but not all, insurance plans that require an authorization to see a counselor will allow you to get an authorization after the fact. You or your therapist can contact the insurance company, let them know when your first appointment was, and the insurance company will approve services from that start date to a specific end date. If you use all of the sessions for which you are approved (it is common for the number of approved sessions to be set somewhere around 10), your counselor or therapist can contact the insurance company to request additional sessions. Some insurance companies will simply approve additional sessions when asked and if basic information is provided, such as the diagnosis, progress made, and approximate length of time needed for continued treatment (e.g., six months, one year). Other insurance companies may require a description from the counselor, indicating that continued treatment is medically necessary (see Question 42). Many times specific mental health diagnoses are identified as being medically necessary. Other times the counselor or therapist must make a case for why a particular diagnosis requires ongoing treatment, which can include the professional's opinion such as what may happen to you as the patient if you were to not receive ongoing mental health care.

As with all services, contacting your insurance company prior to setting up your first appointment is always a good idea. You can confirm whether an authorization is necessary. If it is, you can then ask for how long they approve sessions and for how many sessions. You can also ask what you or your counselor needs to do if more than the approved number of sessions is needed. It is also a good idea to ask if you have to see an in-network provider as part of the approval. If you do, most insurance companies have a website that allows you to search for in-network counselors or psychologists in your area.

44. Why won't my insurance pay for counseling?

There are many possible reasons why your insurance is not paying for your counseling services. It may be as simple as mental health services are not included in your health insurance plan. That can be confirmed by reading through your insurance plan materials, calling the insurance company, or asking your human resources representative if your insurance is purchased through your employer. If the answer is "no," then you know why counseling services aren't or won't be paid for. If the answer is "yes," then there is some other reason the services aren't or won't be paid by the insurance.

Sometimes you or your counselor has submitted incorrect claim information to the insurance company. There is often a specific form that your counselor has to fill out and send to your insurance company in order for them to pay for the service. If the information is filled out incorrectly or a required piece of information (e.g., your date of birth, the diagnosis, your address) is missing, then the claim will be denied. If this is the reason, it is simple enough to fix as long as the counselor or therapist knows what is missing. If your counselor cannot figure it out, they should be able to call the insurance company to get an answer. You can call as well and provide the explanation to your counselor. Similarly, if you are the one submitting claim information and your insurance has not paid for the services, you can call the insurance company directly to find out if you were missing some information or if you provided it in a form that is unacceptable to them.

If you have mental health service coverage, all of the claim-related information was submitted correctly and is complete, and the insurance company is still not paying for services, then it is likely that you have a deductible (see Question 42) that has not been met. Until the deductible has been met, the insurance company will not pay for any portion of the counseling sessions. It is still important for you or your counselor to send claim information to your insurance company as each session submitted is applied toward your deductible, and depending on how large your deductible is, you may eventually meet the deductible and the insurance company will start paying its portion of the service. As implied, though, it is possible that you have a very high deductible (e.g., $5,000), and depending on how many covered services you receive in a year, you may never meet that deductible and therefore the insurance company will never pay for counseling services (and potentially other services).

Another reason your insurance company may not pay for a service is if it determines the service is not medically necessary (see Question 42). If a service is not medically necessary according to your insurance company, it will not pay for the service unless your counselor or therapist can make a case for why the service is medically necessary. This may involve explaining why more sessions than what the insurance company thinks you need is necessary, or why a particular method of treatment for your diagnosis is appropriate. Ultimately, however, the insurance company decides if your treatment is medically necessary or not.

A final reason why your insurance company may not be paying is if you have had a change in insurance or you have not renewed your insurance policy. If the company you work for changes insurance companies and you have not informed your counselor or therapist, claims for your sessions will be denied because they are being sent to the wrong company. Your therapist won't know which the right company is, but they will receive a message indicating that you no longer have the insurance to which they are submitting the claims. A similar message will be generated if you have not renewed your insurance policy. Depending on which one it is, your sessions may or may not be paid for or even covered by the insurance. If you simply forgot to give your counselor the new insurance information, once your counselor has the right information they can submit the claims to the correct insurance plan and, assuming mental health services are covered and you don't have a high deductible, then the insurance company will pay its portion of the session. If, however, you forgot to renew your insurance policy, any sessions you had with your counselor during the period between when your policy ended and when you remembered to renew it will not be paid for or covered by insurance.

❖❖❖

Case Studies

1. GARY FEELS DEPRESSED AND ANXIOUS AND DOESN'T KNOW WHAT TO DO

Gary is a 25-year-old single male who is employed part time and has health insurance through his employer. Growing up Gary never gave much thought to any health-care-related appointments he had since his parents would always schedule them, bring him to them, and pay for them. They never talked with him about health insurance or how to use it other than stating that he should be sure to have health insurance once he is on his own and has a full-time job. His current employer is one he has worked for since he graduated from college. Once he was eligible for health insurance coverage, he purchased a policy and has never had to use it for more than regular health-care checkups with his primary care physician.

Gary has been feeling depressed and anxious for a few months and thought he could "shake it" by going about his regular routine of work, socializing after work and on weekends, and taking care of his dog. His friends have noticed that he has not been his usual "upbeat" self and have asked what is wrong. He usually responds by saying "nothing"; however, since his friends have begun to notice that he does not seem to be his usual self, Gary wondered if there is something really wrong with him and whether he should get help.

Not knowing what to do differently, Gary scheduled an appointment with his primary care provider (PCP) to ask her what to do about how he has been feeling. His PCP noted that she could prescribe an antidepressant or antianxiety medication that may help with his symptoms but that Gary should be evaluated by a mental health professional to confirm if there is a mental health diagnosis. This would also help determine if medication, and which one(s), may be appropriate. Gary asked for recommendations from his PCP for mental health providers in the area and expressed concern about what others may think about him getting help from a "shrink." His PCP reassured him that it is common for people to seek help for mental health concerns and that seeing a counselor would be confidential. Thus, no one would know Gary is seeing a counselor unless he told them that himself.

Gary took the list of mental health professionals provided by his PCP and put them in his wallet where it stayed for several weeks. Gary was hoping that he would not really need to see a mental health professional. He also worried about how much it would cost to see someone. He thought it was one thing to see his PCP once a year for his checkup and occasionally throughout the year when he was sick, but it was another to see someone on a more regular basis and have to shell out the money for each session. He had heard stories from friends who live in other states that their mental health providers charge more than $100 for each session and sometimes up to $250 for each session. Gary decided to hold off on calling any of the names on the list he got from his PCP because he didn't think he could afford it, and he was sure that things would "blow over" soon enough and he'd be back to his old self again.

As time passed Gary realized that he was not feeling better and felt, at times, things were getting even worse. He found that it was more and more difficult for him to get out of bed and get ready for work and that he didn't much feel like playing with his dog. He also found that he was worried a lot. He was particularly worried about work when he was at home and found that he worried about his dog and his social life when he was at work. Gary finally decided to call the first name on the list when he decided to call in sick to work one day even though physically he was fine but he simply did not have the energy to get up and go to work.

Gary left messages with a couple of the names on the list and was able to talk to the third person he called. That therapist asked him several questions, including what led him to make the phone call, what his concerns were, and how long he had been experiencing them. Before ending the call, Gary had an appointment scheduled for the end of the week. After he hung up he realized he had a lot of questions for the therapist, not the least of which was whether he could use his health insurance to see the therapist.

Analysis

Most people know their health insurance helps to pay for medical-related appointments and procedures. Most, though not all, health insurance plans also cover mental health services, which are sometimes referred to as behavioral health services by some insurance companies.

Since Gary did not know what to do when he was not feeling mentally or emotionally well, he made a sound decision by scheduling an appointment with his PCP to get her advice about what to do. It is not always the case that a PCP will recommend that their patient see a mental health professional; however, this does seem to be more and more common place as health-care professionals become more specialized and recognize that professionals in different disciplines can offer effective health care. After getting several names and scheduling an appointment with a therapist, Gary is still left with many questions about how mental health care works, particularly with respect to paying for his sessions.

It would be important for Gary to call the therapist back and verify that the therapist accepts his insurance (e.g., BlueCross/Blue Shield, Medicaid). It is highly likely that the therapist already asked if Gary would be using insurance and, thus, he'd already know the answer to this question. What the therapist will not know, however, is how much of the therapist's fee Gary will have to pay; that answer can be found by calling the health insurance company and/or by looking on his health insurance card. If there are any questions whatsoever, it would be recommended that Gary call customer service at his insurance company, provide the name of the therapist he will be seeing, and inquire about whether sessions are covered if he sees that therapist, how many sessions are covered, whether he needs a referral from his PCP to see the therapist, and how much he will have to pay at each session.

2. KRISTY AND HER RELATIONSHIP WITH HER PARENTS

Kristy is a 16-year-old high school student. She is active in her school through sports and music and has maintained a respectable grade point average. She is socially active as well and has friends from a variety of groups with whom she interacts during "down times" at school, on the weekends, and sometimes during the week in the evenings. Over the past several months Kristy has withdrawn from her current friends and she has participated less actively in her extracurricular activities. Although she does not share with her friends what is going on, she knows she is highly stressed about the relationship between her parents.

Throughout the years Kristy's parents have argued on and off in a way that seemed normal to Kristy. She assumed most parents fought. Recently, however, her parents seemed to fight every time they were together. Previously, the fights between her parents would involve raised voices and each one retreating to a different part of the house. Now, the fights have escalated to the point that both her parents yell at one another, call one another names, and inevitably one of them will leave the house slamming the door behind them, and sometimes not come home for a day or more. When Kristy or her younger brother would ask about what was going on, neither parent provided an answer other than "Nothing, everything is fine. All married couples fight." Sometimes one of them would yell at either Kristy or her brother telling them it is "none of their business."

As the fights escalated, Kristy stayed in her room listening to music through her earbuds as loud as she needed to drown out her parents' fighting. Recently, however, she has not been able to drown them out. This has led to her dreading being at home but not wanting to hang out with her friends either because she didn't want to explain to anyone what was going on—mostly because she didn't know. She would wander around the downtown area where she lived and eventually kept seeing a group of teenagers from her school whom she normally did not talk to. She began encountering them more and more on her walks around town, and eventually she began talking with them and seeking them out when she didn't want to go home. This was a group of teens who were generally categorized as "outcasts" or "druggies." Not all of them used drugs, but all of them smoked cigarettes and did not participate in extracurricular activities of any kind.

As Kristy got to know the teens in this group, she realized she didn't have much in common with them except for the fact that they would all sometimes complain about how miserable their homelives were, particularly in regard to their parents. Kristy began sharing some of her experiences with her own parents with those in this group. On one occasion, one of the teens in the group offered Kristy a joint. She smoked it and found that she felt somewhat better but mostly that her worries and problems didn't really seem to bother her as much. Once her high wore off, she was painfully aware of what her homelife was like and found that she was seeking this group out as often as possible, including during school.

Kristy started hanging out with them on more occasions, which led to her being offered more than just marijuana. She was offered beer, hard liquor, and harder drugs such as cocaine and opioids. She experimented with everything they offered her and found that each substance helped her to forget or at least not care, and overall, she felt better as long as she was under the influence of some substance. Kristy began skipping out on music or athletic practice and was often late to school or did not go altogether. She tried to keep all of this from her parents by pretending to go to school and pretending to stay after school in order to participate in whatever extracurricular activity she had been going to. Eventually, however, her parents were informed of her absences, her slipping grades, and the fact that she was going to get kicked out of her activities if she did not start showing up again.

Kristy's parents demanded to know what was going on and told her that she had to see a counselor. Kristy's friends too, although growing more estranged, expressed concern and wondered if she needed to talk to someone. A part of her thought it might be a good idea to see a counselor because she knew what she was doing was not really okay, but another part of her didn't really care and, more important, did not want to share what was really going on with a counselor because her parents would then know what she had been up to.

Analysis

Kristy seems to be strongly and negatively affected by the nature of her parents' relationship. In order to cope with the stress her parents' fighting has caused her, she first withdrew from those closest to her and found ways to be out of the house as much as possible. Eventually, this led her to connect with a group of students with whom she would not have normally connected. They were the kids with a reputation for being socially disconnected from "mainstream" students and school activities and with a reputation for drug use. Kristy was initially drawn to them due to their shared experiences of having a tumultuous homelife. Eventually, Kristy found that the drugs offered to her provided her with an escape that nothing else had provided her to that point.

As Kristy began to engage in more self-destructive behavior, she further disengaged from her normal activities and from putting forth effort with her schoolwork, all of which caught the attention of school personnel, her friends, and, eventually, her parents. Although Kristy is reluctant to see a counselor, ideally, she would find someone she could talk to who could reassure her of the benefits of talking with someone who is not involved directly in what is going on in her life. It would also be important for Kristy to know that seeing a licensed mental health provider would probably mean that they would not be able to reveal to her parents what they talk about. In some states, a client who is at least 16 years old (in other states the age may be younger or older) can expect confidentiality around issues such as drugs and alcohol and sexual activity. Knowing this might reassure Kristy that she can discuss what she needs to without fear of things getting back to her parents. Of course, it would be important for Kristy to inquire with her counselor about the limits to confidentiality, particularly with respect to her parents. Should Kristy start seeing a counselor it is possible that the counselor may also recommend family therapy since Kristy is distressed by what is happening in the home between her parents, or couples counseling for the parents specifically.

3. JENNA AND MARK TRY MARRIAGE COUNSELING

Jenna and Mark have been married for seven years and have two children, with a third on the way. Their marriage, like many marriages, started out very well. Prior to having their first child they seemed to communicate effectively and had a good time together watching movies and going out with friends. The birth of their first child was stressful, but they both chalked that up to not getting enough sleep due to the baby not sleeping through the night. As their first child grew up and things became easier due to the baby getting into a regular sleep routine, and being able to do more and more things on her own like feeding herself and playing by herself, Jenna and Mark agreed that their marriage was still strong and that the stress they felt previously had been situational and predominantly due to lack of sleep.

After the birth of their second child, Jenna and Mark went through a similar set of experiences, with the new baby not sleeping through the night, but this time they had another child to take care of and who seemed to be "going backwards" by wetting the bed and sucking her thumb again. Jenna and Mark recognized that they were fighting more again but that they seemed to be fighting more than they did than with the first baby. Both wondered if their disagreements were not really about sleep deprivation but about something else that was not working between them. They occasionally talked about this, but with two young children to care for and both of them working, they barely had time and energy to take care of the basics, let alone attend to complex relationship issues. As such, they seemed to adopt an unspoken agreement that they did not really need to talk about things anyway since their relationship started out strong it must still be strong.

As their children grew older and they had more time together, Jenna and Mark found that they were still too tired to put much effort into things beyond taking care of the kids, the house, the cars, and responsibilities related to their job. They occasionally tried to commit to watching a movie together like they used to; however, one of two things would happen. One of them would fall asleep in the middle of the movie, or they could not agree on what movie to watch. They were cordial to one another but found that they talked less and less with one another apart from catching each other up on what was done that day and what still needed to be done.

During the past two years of their marriage they found that they struggled to talk with one another about things that were important to them unrelated to day-to-day responsibilities. When they tried to share what they thought about and wished for themselves individually and as a couple, both felt the other wasn't really listening and didn't really understand. The result was that they both avoided one another when there was time to really sit and talk. They tended to spend their downtime in different parts of the house and found that they were arguing more and more over the "little things" that "didn't really matter."

Despite their growing emotional distance, Jenna and Mark decided to have another baby, both thinking that caring for another child would bring them closer together. Although the baby has not yet been born, the strain on their marriage has increased. They fight about how to pay for the increased costs of having another child, they fight about whether this child will sleep in bed with them while the child is still nursing, and they fight about household chores, including whether they are shared equally.

One evening, following a fight about who would empty the dishwasher, Mark told Jenna that he had had it and that he didn't think their marriage could be saved. This caught Jenna by surprise as she thought they were struggling but didn't think they were on the verge of divorce. Mark said he had been thinking about the possibility of divorce for some time but didn't want to bring it up because he didn't want to fight about yet another thing. Jenna was angry that she was "kept in the dark" about this and suggested that they should see a marriage counselor before making any kind of decision about their marriage. She said that she was sure they could save it since they had been close and happy in the beginning of their marriage. The next day Jenna scheduled an appointment with a marriage counselor and told Mark when it was. He was furious that she scheduled it, saying that he refused to talk to a counselor and didn't think their marriage could be saved anyway.

Analysis

Jenna is left with a dilemma about what to do with respect to the appointment she scheduled. It is possible that Mark may change his mind by the time of the appointment; however, it is equally likely that he will refuse to go; thus, Jenna has to decide whether to cancel the appointment.

It would be a good idea for Jenna to find out from Mark if there are any circumstances under which he would go to a marriage counselor. If there is not, then it would be a good idea for Jenna to call the marriage counselor and let him or her know what the current situation is. It is possible that the counselor may be able to give Jenna some advice on what she can say to encourage Mark to reconsider going. For example, sometimes marriage counseling is effective in repairing a marriage, and sometimes this type of counseling is effective in helping couples figure out how to separate in a mutually beneficial way, particularly since there are children involved. Assuming Mark remains disinterested in going to counseling, the counselor may encourage Jenna to keep the appointment in the event of a last-minute change of mind so that she can get some support on her own.

Should Jenna end up attending the marriage counselor on her own, she may or may not be able to keep seeing this counselor. He may work only with couples, or he may also take on individual clients, and in that case, he and Jenna could decide if she would like to see him on an individual basis so she can get support while going through what may be the dissolution of her marriage.

4. DARREN WANTS TO FIND A NEW THERAPIST

Darren is a 20-year-old college student, who recently started counseling for issues related to depression and anxiety. He has dealt with depression or anxiety much of his life and saw counselors on and off throughout his childhood and into early adolescence. His parents made him go to counseling when he was younger, so they set up all of his appointments and selected his counselors. Darren agreed that counseling had helped him, but as he got older, and was feeling better, he started to complain about having to go. He insisted to his parents that he was fine and that what would help him now is to spend the time he'd be going to the counselor on things he enjoys. His symptoms remained at bay for the better part of a year but slowly started to return during his first year in college. He was able to manage on his own because he was able to look forward to the various breaks and vacations that occurred during the school year and viewed these times away from academics as a form of therapy.

Toward the end of his junior year and into his senior year of college, Darren's symptoms returned and started to interfere not only with his overall happiness and well-being but also with his schoolwork. He made it through his junior year and passed all of his classes, but that was only because he had done so well early in each semester. Without high-enough grades early on, Darren would have failed most of his classes. He convinced himself, again, that all he needed was time away from the pressures of school and the looming expectation of graduation and the start of his career.

Darren did feel better over the summer. He was able to spend time with his friends and do things that were enjoyable to him. He had a full-time job, but it was low pressure and did not require much beyond Darren showing up and doing what was asked of him. Thus, his job was not a significant source of stress and provided money for him to be able to spend his free time doing whatever he wanted. In retrospect, Darren realized that although he did feel much better throughout the summer, he was not fully himself. He felt down on and off throughout most weeks and dealt with the occasional bout of anxiety though he did not know what he was anxious about.

At the end of the summer when it was time to return to school, Darren felt excited to go back as he usually did. He was looking forward to seeing his college friends again and looking forward to completing his final year of college. Darren, admittedly, did not know exactly what he was going to do once he graduated. He realized this thought did cause him some anxiety, but he was able to push it aside by telling himself that he'd figure it out since that was what senior year was all about.

Darren's return to school was as he expected. The first couple of weeks were filled with spending time with friends, hanging out, going to parties, and very little high-stakes homework or exams since it was so early in the semester. After the following couple of weeks of the semester, Darren started to feel the pressure of maintaining his social relationships and keeping up with his schoolwork. He realized that all he wanted to do was to hang out with his friends so he would procrastinate getting his work done, which only made him feel worse. He talked with his friends about it in as lighthearted a way as possible, and they all laughed and agreed that they all procrastinate. Darren noticed, however, that they did not seem to be as bothered by it as he was, and after a couple more weeks of putting things off and feeling stressed about getting everything done, he realized he was starting to feel just as he did when he was a kid.

Since Darren had previously had good experiences with counselors, he called the campus counseling center and set up an appointment as early

as possible. He met with his counselor and described his current concerns
as best as he could and provided information about his history of depression and anxiety along with what it was for him seeing a counselor at that
time. After a few sessions, Darren felt he was not getting what he needed
from his counselor. She was nice and seemed to care, but he wasn't feeling
better, and Darren felt she was not able to truly understand him and how
he was feeling. She offered Darren a referral for medication, saying that he
would likely feel better if he were prescribed something for his depression
and anxiety-related symptoms. Darren didn't feel he needed or wanted
medication; rather, he wanted to work through things as he had with his
previous therapists. Darren decided he wanted to see a different counselor
but didn't know how do go about it or if that was even allowed.

Analysis

Darren's situation is not that uncommon, in terms of not only waiting
until things feel "bad enough" to seek counseling but also that his counselor may not be a good fit for him. Since Darren has been in counseling
before, albeit as a child or adolescent, he is probably able to determine
whether therapy is working for him. It is difficult, however, after only a
few sessions to know for sure if the counselor or therapist with whom one
is working is truly not a good fit.

Initially it may be good for Darren to give it another session or two
with his current counselor to see if things feel better. Sometimes it can
take more than a few sessions to truly feel comfortable with a counselor.
It would also be helpful for Darren to let his counselor know that he
is not getting what he needs. This can be as simple as saying just that.
Then Darren and the counselor can further discuss this and explore why
counseling does not feel like it is working. It could be that his counselor's
approach is different from what he is used to and his counselor's explanation of how she goes about treatment may help Darren see their work
together differently.

If, however, this does not work or Darren does not want to spend
another session or two trying to figure this out, it is perfectly acceptable to
change therapists. He would not have to give a reason for wanting such
a change, although his counselor may ask. Sometimes clients simply stop
showing up or stop scheduling appointments; however, if possible, talking
with the counselor about wanting to make a change can mean Darren is
able to say what he needs in a counselor (if he knows) and the counselor
can make a recommendation based on his preferences.

5. SARAH HAS BEHAVIORAL ISSUES

Sarah is an eight-year-old girl, who lives with her parents and a younger brother. She is currently in third grade, and her brother is in kindergarten at the same school Sarah attends. Sarah started to show behavior problems during the second grade; however, prior to that time Sarah seemed to be a well-adjusted child who was happy at school and happy at home. The only indication that Sarah may have had some struggles was when her younger brother was born when she was two years old. Sarah showed some signs of regression (e.g., sucking her thumb again after having stopped for a year and wanting to be rocked to sleep at night which she had not previously needed except for when she was a new infant). After several months, Sarah seemed to adjust to having a new sibling, and her need to suck her thumb and to be rocked to sleep at night discontinued.

Currently, Sarah has been lashing out at friends, teachers, and family members when she feels frustrated. This started when she was in the second grade, but the number of times Sarah expressed frustration by lashing out was sporadic and limited to a handful of occasions. Both Sarah's parents and teachers explained this by some unknown stressor that may have affected Sarah, but that was not obvious to others. About a month or so into her third-grade year, Sarah began showing more frequent signs of frustration with herself and her classmates. When she did not get what she wanted (e.g., a turn on a swing soon enough during recess or having to share crayons during art class), Sarah was quick to yell at anyone she thought was keeping her from getting what she wanted and would say they were "stupid" or "mean." Most recently, Sarah had expressed her frustration physically by hitting or pushing others. Although she never hit or pushed a teacher, she began calling them stupid or mean if she thought the teachers did not take her side.

Sarah has been sent to the principal's office several times per week in the past three weeks, but her behavior has not seemed to decrease. Sarah agreed that what she was doing was not "nice" and that it was "wrong" but that she did not feel she could stop herself. She began meeting with the school counselor on a weekly basis and had more regular "check-ins" to see how she was doing throughout the week. Although the school counselor was able to help Sarah identify what made her frustrated while she was at school, the counselor was unable to help Sarah stop these behaviors.

Since Sarah has been showing more signs of aggressive behavior toward nearly anyone who might "get in her way," Sarah has lost some friendships, which has also made her more withdrawn from others. Although Sarah blames her friends for being mean and not caring about her when asked by the school counselor, these kids indicate that they would still want to be friends with Sarah if *she* "weren't so mean anymore."

The school counselor and the principal have regularly been in contact with and met with Sarah's parents to explain what has been happening at school. At the most recent meeting the principal indicated that Sarah likely needs more support than the school can provide and that without the additional support Sarah may not be able to continue to attend the school since her behavior has been disruptive and increasingly aggressive. They all agreed that seeing a mental health counselor who specializes in working with children who show signs of aggressiveness would be warranted. The school counselor provided Sarah's parents with a list of names of local licensed mental health providers, and they scheduled an appointment with one of them.

After meeting with the new counselor Sarah told her parents that she liked the counselor but didn't really think she needed to see one. Her parents reassured her that the counselor could help Sarah cope with her feelings of frustration in a way that would allow her to keep her friendships and make new ones. They also explained that if she was not able to learn how to control her behavior she might not be able to keep going to school there, to which Sarah responded with intense frustration, stating that she hated the school and everyone there anyway and that she hated her parents for making her go to counseling and for not being on her side.

After several sessions of getting to know Sarah and how she feels about herself, her family, her peers, and her life in general, the counselor recommended to Sarah's parents that in addition to individual counseling for Sarah she would recommend family counseling for the entire family (i.e., Sarah, her parents, and possibly her brother). The counselor provided names of licensed family therapists to Sarah's parents and recommended that they set something up as soon as possible. Although Sarah's parents intend to follow through on this recommendation, they were unclear why they and their son needed to go to therapy since Sarah was the one struggling to control her behavior.

Analysis

Without additional information it is not known what may or may not be going on at home that may be contributing to Sarah's new struggle with frustration tolerance. It is not uncommon for children to act out in this way when there are stressors at home such as marital discord between parents or other stressors such as financial problems, a death in the family, or the loss of a pet. In this case, having family therapy provides an opportunity to discuss how any stressors may affect the entire family and how each family member may cope with such stressors in a different way. The parents can learn how their ability or inability to effectively cope with a stressor might inadvertently affect their children, and they can learn how to cope differently as well as how to help each child cope in an adaptive way.

It is also possible that it is not a family stressor that is the cause of Sarah's new, disruptive behavior. It may be that she is going through a particularly difficult developmental stage or that there is something going on at school that has not yet been identified (e.g., bullying). Regardless of the reason or whether or not the reason can be identified, family therapy can help all members learn how to communicate more effectively. In addition, family therapy can provide an opportunity for each family member to talk about how they affect one another both when they are feeling and behaving well and when they are feeling or behaving badly. Sarah's parents can learn effective strategies for supporting both of their children when either are struggling and how to manage their own stress, particularly when they are worried about how their children are doing.

Glossary

At risk: a term that refers to someone who is exposed to harm or danger and therefore is at risk of being hurt. In the context of counseling and therapy, those who are at risk are those who are more susceptible to psychological and/or physical harm due to their circumstances, genetics, or personal belief systems and are, therefore, at risk for a mental illness.

Authorization: an insurance term that refers to the permission a client and their therapist may need from the insurance company prior to starting or continuing a therapy relationship. Some insurance companies will authorize a certain number of sessions (e.g., eight sessions) for a certain period of time (e.g., from January 1 to June 30 of that calendar year). When the time frame is up or the number of sessions has been used, an additional authorization for more sessions must be obtained.

Behavior therapy: a treatment approach designed to help clients change their behaviors using the principles of learning such as those associated with classical conditioning, operant conditioning, and observational learning. The assumption from this approach is that all behavior is learned and, therefore, unhealthy behaviors can be unlearned and replaced by new, healthier learned behaviors.

Classical conditioning: a theory of learning that states when two stimuli are associated or paired consistently enough, any behavior that occurs as a result of the second stimulus will occur with the first. For example, a dog salivates naturally in the presence of food. When the presence of food is preceded by the sound of a bell (i.e., the bell is rung then the food is presented), the dog will eventually learn that the bell and the food go together and will start salivating to the sound of the bell.

Cognitive behavioral therapy (CBT): an approach to the treatment of mental illness that assumes problems are based on faulty thinking and of behaviors that cause distress. Treatment using CBT involves helping patients learn more adaptive ways of thinking and healthier behaviors.

Coinsurance: an insurance term that refers to a percentage of the counselor's fee (e.g., 20%) that the client is responsible for paying. The insurance company pays the remaining percentage.

Common factors: in the context of therapy, common factors are those things that are believed to exist in all types of therapy (e.g., psychodynamic, cognitive behavioral) and are believed to be important for explaining why therapy works. Some common factors include empathy, the working alliance (i.e., the relationship between the client and therapist), and expectations about whether therapy will work.

Confidentiality: a legal and ethical term that refers to the fact that a counselor or therapist cannot reveal any aspect of someone's counseling services (including the fact that they are in counseling) to anyone without first receiving permission from the client. There are exceptions to this, which include when the client is a threat to themselves or someone else, when a counselor is court-ordered to reveal information, and/or the client sues their counselor for any reason.

Co-payment (co-pay): an insurance term that refers to a dollar amount (e.g., $20.00) of the counselor's fee that the client is responsible for paying. The insurance company pays the remainder of the fee.

Counselor: in the context of mental health, a counselor is a professional who may or may not have a license to diagnose and treat mental illness but is trained to offer guidance related to distress in a client's life.

Deductible: an insurance term that refers to the amount of money someone has to pay before the insurance company will begin paying for all or a portion of health-care services, including therapy.

Diagnostic and Statistical Manual of Mental Disorders-5 (DSM-5): a manual published by the American Psychiatric Association that includes all psychiatric diagnoses, their symptoms, typical presentations, and a summary of research related to the diagnosis.

Diathesis-stress model: an approach that explains psychological symptoms in the context of both someone's biology and environment. The idea is that we are all predisposed (genetically) to various problems, which is the diathesis part of the model, and that the "right" environment, which is the stress part of the model, creates the situation in which our particular vulnerability may arise. In short, one will not develop a psychological (or medical) problem if one does not have the genetics for it *and* the right environment that triggers the problem to develop.

Eclectic therapy: an approach to mental health treatment that incorporates elements of various other approaches (e.g., cognitive behavioral therapy, psychodynamic psychotherapy) in order to best meet the needs of a client.

Evidence-based practice: refers to providing treatment that is based on existing scientific research, the therapist's experience, and who the client is, including their culture and preferences.

Family therapy: a mode of therapy that involves one or two therapists and members of a family, which may or may not include those who live in the same household, for the purpose of helping the family function as effectively as possible.

Genogram: an intricate family tree that includes not only which family members are connected to others but also how they are connected (e.g., twins, married, divorced), the nature of the connection (e.g., distant, very close, physical abuse), and any important issues that members of the family may be dealing with (e.g., anger problem, substance abuse, depression). Specific symbols and notations are used to indicate these items (e.g., squares or circles, dashed lines, double lines).

Group therapy: a mode of therapy in which a group of 5–15 people with similar concerns meet with one or two therapists to share experiences, learn how to more effectively communicate, and how to develop satisfying interpersonal relationships.

Health Insurance Portability and Accountability Act (HIPAA): a federal law that states how a client's health-related information should be stored and transmitted in order to ensure a client's privacy.

In-network: an insurance term that refers to health-care providers who have signed a contract with an insurance company to provide services for which they are licensed (e.g., mental health services) at a rate agreed on by the insurance company and the provider.

Inpatient treatment: refers to treatment that takes place in a hospital setting when the patient has been admitted to stay at hospital to receive treatment.

Intake session: an initial session with either a counselor/therapist or an intake specialist who will gather demographic information along with information about current symptoms, history of symptoms, history of past treatments, medications taken, and so on.

Interpersonal psychotherapy: a time-limited therapy (i.e., a certain number of sessions) that focuses on a client's interpersonal relationships. The form of therapy takes the perspective that the nature of a patient's interpersonal relationships is what causes and perpetuates psychological distress.

Mental health diagnosis: a formal diagnosis of a mental health concern typically using the *Diagnostic and Statistical Manual of Mental Disorders* (*DSM*) to render such a diagnosis. A mental health concern that is diagnosable usually affects someone's mood, thinking, and behavior.

Observational learning: a theory of learning that states an observer will change his or her behavior after observing another person's behavior (i.e., a model or role model) and the consequences of their behavior. For example, if a child observes an older sibling getting punished for staying out too late, the young child may not do that in the future, whereas behaviors that are reinforced or rewarded, and observed by the younger child, are more likely to be imitated by that child.

Off-label prescriptions: refers to medications that are prescribed to treat a disorder for which the medication has not been formally tested or formally approved by the U.S. Food and Drug Administration (FDA).

Operant conditioning: a theory of learning that states behaviors that are reinforced or rewarded are more likely to occur again and behaviors that are punished are less likely to occur again.

Out-of-network: an insurance term that refers to a health-care provider who is qualified to provide the treatment needed but has not contracted with the insurance company to provide services. The client can still see an out-of-network provider but will likely have to pay more per session than if they were seeing an in-network provider.

Outpatient treatment: this is treatment that takes place outside of a hospital or residential treatment setting.

Primary care provider (PCP): your PCP is the medical provider you see for regular medical checkups and with whom you schedule appointments when you are not feeling well. Some insurances require that your PCP make a referral to a licensed mental health-care provider before you can see them.

Psychiatrist: refers to a physician who has a particular specialty in psychiatry. Specializing in psychiatry means that a psychiatrist has the same basic education as any physician but devoted much of their education, training, and supervision to the diagnosis and treatment of mental health issues.

Psychoanalytic psychotherapy: a form of insight-oriented therapy that emphasizes the unconscious mind and its impact on the psychological functioning of patients. This form of psychotherapy was developed by Sigmund Freud and involves using free association (i.e., saying whatever comes to mind) and dream analysis to uncover unconscious desires and wishes.

Psychodynamic psychotherapy: an insight-oriented therapy that is based on psychoanalytic psychotherapy. The primary differences have to do with the fact that this form of therapy does not occur as frequently or for as long as psychoanalytic psychotherapy and the techniques used are not necessarily the same.

Psychological testing: this is testing conducted by a psychologist or someone under the supervision of a psychologist for the purpose of diagnosis, treatment recommendations, or recommended accommodations for work or school. This type of testing often involves testing related to intelligence, achievement, personality, attention and hyperactivity, behavior at home and school, and so on.

Psychologist: refers to someone who has completed graduate-level training in the area of psychology. Usually a psychologist has a doctoral-level degree (i.e., PhD or PsyD); however, in some instances clinicians with a master's degree (i.e., MA or MS) may be allowed to call themselves a psychologist. Not all psychologists are licensed to provide mental health services; however, if you are seeking mental health services and have found a psychologist offering such services, they should be licensed to do so.

Psychotropic medications: the term used to indicate that a medication is prescribed for the purpose of treating a mental health diagnosis.

Referral: a referral is usually made from one professional to another for the purpose of connecting clients with other professionals who can provide the services needed or recommended. Some insurance companies require a formal referral (usually from your primary care provider [PCP]) before they will cover the services.

Release of information (ROI): refers to the permission you give to a provider to share information with or to get information from another provider or other interested party. Permission can be given verbally; however, it is best to provide this kind of permission in writing. Clients can revoke this release at any time for any reason.

Specialty: refers to education, training, and supervision in a particular area of service. Clinicians can have a specialty with certain age groups, diagnoses, type of therapy (e.g., cognitive behavioral therapy), sexual orientation, unique populations (e.g., athletes), and so on. Some professional organizations provide certification for particular specialties, which means the provider has met their standards for education, training, and supervision in that specialty area.

Supportive psychotherapy: a form of psychotherapy that was originally used by psychoanalysts when patients were incapable of engaging as needed for psychoanalysis to work. Currently, supportive psychotherapy is an effective form of therapy that can be used with a wide variety of patients. The focus of this approach is on the therapeutic alliance and using this relationship to help improve symptoms and self-esteem in the patient.

Systematic desensitization: a behavioral intervention that involves systematically desensitizing a patient to their fear or phobia. This form of treatment involves having a fear hierarchy of the object or situation that is feared, and the patient is exposed to the lowest level of the hierarchy until the patient either feels reasonably relaxed or does not feel debilitating anxiety. Once that occurs, the patient is exposed to the next level of the hierarchy and so on until the top level of the hierarchy (i.e., the item at this level induces the greatest amount of fear or anxiety) is reached.

Therapeutic alliance: the connection that the patient feels with his or her counselor or therapist. As part of this alliance, the patient feels that his or her counselor has the same goals, respects the patient and his or her experiences, and views the patient positively.

Therapist: a term that is short for psychotherapist and is often used interchangeably with counselor. Technically, a therapist or psychotherapist is trained to provide in-depth, insight-oriented services designed to help clients develop a better understanding of themselves and their thoughts, feelings, and behaviors.

Directory of Resources

ORGANIZATIONS

American Association for Marriage and Family Therapy (AAMFT)

https://www.aamft.org/

The American Association for Marriage and Family Therapy is a professional organization with over 50,000 members who are professionals in or students of the field of marriage and family therapy. The mission of the AAMFT is to support the field of marriage and family therapy as well as to support the well-being of individuals, couples, families, and the communities in which they live.

American Counseling Association (ACA)

https://www.counseling.org/

The American Counseling Association was founded in 1952 based on shared interests of four professional associations that existed at that time and formally adopted the association's current name in 1992. The ACA functions to not only support the field of counseling but also ensure individuals who seek support from counselors are effectively aided in their pursuit of mental health, wellness, education, and career goals.

American Group Psychotherapy Association (AGPA)

https://www.agpa.org/

The American Group Psychotherapy Association was formed for professionals interested in and practicing group psychotherapy. It is a multidisciplinary association with 3,000 members and functions to inform the public at large about the existence and benefits of group psychotherapy. It also offers qualified practicing professionals the credential *certified group psychotherapist*.

American Psychiatric Association (APA)

https://www.psychiatry.org/

The American Psychiatric Association claims to be the leading psychiatric organization worldwide and has over 37,000 members. Its mission is to ensure that individuals and their families have access to high-quality psychiatric care, to support education and research in the field of psychiatry, and to support the needs of its professional members.

American Psychological Association (APA)

http://www.apa.org/

The American Psychological Association has over 115,000 members who are students, researchers, educators, clinicians, and consultants in the field of psychology. Its mission is to promote the application of psychology to every aspect of human life by educating the public through reports, publications, meetings, and professional connections; to promote psychological research and the field as a science; and to ensure the highest quality of care provided by psychologists.

National Association of Social Workers (NASW)

https://www.socialworkers.org/

The National Association of Social Workers was founded in 1955 and claims to be the largest professional association of social workers worldwide with over 120,000 members. The organization advocates for sound public policy that ensures the health, welfare, and education of individuals and their families, and it ensures a high quality of care provided by social workers.

WEBSITES

American Association for Marriage and Family Therapy Code of Ethics

https://www.aamft.org/Legal_Ethics/Code_of_Ethics.aspx

American Counseling Association Ethical and Professional Standards

https://www.counseling.org/knowledge-center/ethics

American Psychological Association's Ethical Principles of Psychologists and Code of Conduct

https://www.apa.org/ethics/code/

HIPAA for Individuals

https://www.hhs.gov/hipaa/for-individuals/index.html

National Association of Social Workers Code of Ethics

https://www.socialworkers.org/about/ethics/code-of-ethics

Privacy, Security, and Electronic Health Records (pdf)

https://www.hhs.gov/sites/default/files/ocr/privacy/hipaa/understanding/
consumers/privacy-security-electronic-records.pdf

Sharing Health Information with Family Members and Friends (pdf)

https://www.hhs.gov/sites/default/files/ocr/privacy/hipaa/understanding/
consumers/sharing-family-friends.pdf

Your Health Information Privacy Rights (pdf)

https://www.hhs.gov/sites/default/files/ocr/privacy/hipaa/understanding/
consumers/consumer_rights.pdf

Index

About the Author

Christine L. B. Selby is a licensed psychologist, sport psychologist, and eating disorder specialist. She is also associate professor of psychology at Husson University and maintains a part-time private practice with Selby Psychological Services, PLLC. She is a certified eating disorder specialist with the International Association of Eating Disorders Professionals (iaedp™) and was the cofounder (2008) and cochair (2008–2014) of the Eating Disorders Special Interest Group of the Association for Applied Sport Psychology. Dr. Selby has published articles and book chapters in the area of eating disorders in athletes. She has also presented locally and nationally on eating disorders and related topics at professional conferences and to allied professionals who work directly with those dealing with eating disorders and related concerns. Dr. Selby is the author of *Chilling Out: The Psychology of Relaxation, The Body Size and Health Debate, Obesity: Your Questions Answered*, and *The Psychology of Eating Disorders*.